TAXMANN'S

UNDERSTANDING NEW CRIMINAL LAWS

TAXMANN®'S

Understanding New CRIMINAL LAWS

July 2024

Price : ₹ 175

Published by :
Taxmann Publications (P.) Ltd.

Sales & Marketing :
59/32, New Rohtak Road, New Delhi-110 005 India
Phone : +91-11-45562222
Website : www.taxmann.com
E-mail : sales@taxmann.com

Regd. Office :
21/35, West Punjabi Bagh, New Delhi-110 026 India

Printed at :
Tan Prints (India) Pvt. Ltd.
44 Km. Mile Stone, National Highway, Rohtak Road
Village Rohad, Distt. Jhajjar (Haryana) India
E-mail : sales@tanprints.com

CONTENTS

PAGE

DIVISION THREE

UNDERSTANDING LAW OF EVIDENCE UNDER BHARATIYA SAKSHYA ADHINIYAM, 2023 (BSA)

DIVISION ONE

UNDERSTANDING OFFENCES AND PUNISHMENT UNDER BHARATIYA NYAYA SANHITA, 2023 (BNS)

ALPHABETICAL KEY TO UNDERSTANDING OFFENCES AND PUNISHMENT UNDER BHARATIYA NYAYA SANHITA, 2023 (BNS)

Aadhaar card, forgery of, ***para 1.1***

- Aadhaar Card

Abetment outside india for offence committed in India, ***para 1.2***

- Abatement outside India

Adultery, ***para 1.3***

- Adultery

Beggary, ***para 1.4***

- Beggary

Black marketing of cinema/match tickets, ***para 1.5***

- Black marketing of tickets
- Punishability of Ticket scalping or ticket touting was grey area under IPC
- Unauthorised selling of tickets by a member of a group or gang is punishable as petty organised crime under BNS
- Meaning of "unauthorised selling of tickets"

Breach of peace, intentional insult with intent to provoke, ***para 1.6***

- Mandatory Summary trial

Causing death by negligence, ***para 1.7***

- Increased punishment

Cheating, ***para 1.8***

- Prescribed punishment
- When offence of cheating is punishable under this section and when punishable u/s 112

Child, ***para 1.9***

- Child

Child, hiring, employing or engaging to commit an offence, ***para 1.10***

- Hiring child to commit an offence

Civil recovery of proceeds of crime and distribution to victims of crime, ***para 1.11***

- Civil recovery

Coin, currency-notes, bank notes and government stamps, offences relating to - Possession of forged or counterfeit coins, government stamp, currency-notes or bank-notes, ***para 1.12***

- Possession of counterfeit currency

Community service, ***para 1.13***

- Community Service
- Offences for which punishment of community service can be awarded

Community service/payment of fine, default of, ***para 1.14***

- Community service
- Default in payment of fine or default of community service

Construction, negligent conduct with respect to pulling down, repairing or constructing buildings, etc., ***para 1.15***

- Scope of provision
- Prescribed fine

Counterfeit seal etc., making or possessing, with intent to commit forgery punishable under section 338, ***para 1.16***

- Counterfeiting

Damage to government property, ***para 1.17***

- Damage to Government property

Defamation, ***para 1.18***

- Any manner
- Community service

Document, ***para 1.19***

Drunken person, misconduct in public by, ***para 1.20***

- Community service

Forfeiture of property, *para 1.21*

- Forfeiture of property
- New provision of section 107 of BNSS provides that proceeds of crime will be distributed among victims and unclaimed amount will be forfeited to Govt.
- Attachment of property derived or obtained, directly or indirectly, as a result of a criminal activity or from the commission of any offence
- Procedure for attachment of properties which are proceeds of crime
- Rateable distribution of attached/seized among victims of crime if attached/seized properties found to be proceeds of crime
- Proceeds of crime to be forfeited to government if no claimants to receive such proceeds

Forgery of voter identity card, *para 1.22*

- Voter-Id Card

Gender, *para 1.23*

- Transgender recognised as gender and defined

Grievous hurt, voluntarily causing, *para 1.24*

- Causing permanent disability
- Mob lynching - Grievous hurt

Hit and run cases, *para 1.25*

- Increased punishment
- Offender escaping or failing to report

Kidnapping or maiming a child for purpose of begging, *para 1.26*

- Prescribed punishment
- Child

Life imprisonment, *para 1.27*

- Life imprisonment

Medical practitioner causing death by his negligent act in medical procedure, *para 1.28*

- Death caused by Medical practitioner's negligence in performing medical procedure
- Definition of "Registered Medical Practitioner"

Mob lynching - death, *para 1.29*

- Mob Lynching (Death)

Mob lynching (hurt or grievous hurt), ***para 1.30***

- Mob lynching (hurt/grievous hurt)

Month and year, ***para 1.31***

- Reference to British calendar replaced with reference to Gregorian calendar

Movable property, ***para 1.32***

- Scope of "Movable property" in section 2(*21*) not limited to property in corporeal form, unlike the definition in section 22
- Impact of changes in definition of movable property

National integration, imputations, assertions prejudicial to, ***para 1.33***

- Electronic communication
- False information

Organised crime, ***para 1.34***

- Organised Crime
- Definition of "Continuing unlawful activity" [Clause *(ii)* of *Explanation* below Section 111(1)]
- Definition of "Economic offence" [Clause *(iii)* of *Explanation* below Section 111(1)]
- Continuing unlawful activity/Economic offence/other unlawful activity
- New definition of "Organised crime syndicate" [Clause *(i)* of *Explanation* below Section 111(1)]
- Punishment for committing organized crime [Section 111(2)]
- Punishment for abetment of, attempt to commit, or facilitating organized crime or engaging in activity preparatory to organized crime [Section 111(3)]
- Punishment for being a member of an organized crime syndicate [Section 111(4)]
- Punishment for intentionally harbouring or concealing any person who has committed the offence of an organised crime [Section 111(5)]
- Punishment for possession of any property derived or obtained from the commission of an organised crime or proceeds of any organised crime or which has been acquired through the organised crime [Section 111(6)]

- Punishment for person in possession of any property on behalf of a member of an organized crime syndicate which he cannot satisfactorily account for [Section 111(7)]

Organised crime, petty, ***para 1.35***

- Definition of "petty organized crime" [Section 112(2)]
- Scope of the term "theft" [*Explanation* to section 112(1)]
- Punishment for petty organized crime
- When offence of theft is punishable under this section and when punishable u/s 303 of BNS
- When offence of snatching is punishable under this section and when punishable u/s 304 of BNS
- When offence of cheating is punishable under this section and when punishable u/s 318
- When offence of theft from vehicle, dwelling house or business premises is punishable under this section and when punishable u/s 305

Proclaimed offender, non-appearance in response to a proclamation under section 84 of BNSS, 2023, ***para 1.36***

- Community service
- Scope of "proclaimed offenders" expanded by section 84 of BNSS
- Joint Trial

Promoting enmity between different groups on grounds of religion, race, place of birth, residency, language, etc., and doing acts prejudicial to maintenance of harmony, ***para 1.37***

- Electronic communication

Public servant, assaulting or obstructing when suppressing riot, etc., ***para 1.38***

- Scope of provisions
- Prescribed punishment

Public servant unlawfully engaging in trade, ***para 1.39***

- Community Service

Publishing false or misleading information to jeopardize sovereignty unity and Integrity or security of India, ***para 1.40***

- Electronic communication
- False information

Terrorist Act, ***para 1.49***

- BNS *v.* UAPA
- Police officer of rank of SP and above to decide whether offence to be registered under UAPA or under this section
- Definition of 'terrorist act'
- Punishment for commission of 'terrorist act' [Section 113(2)]
- Punishment for conspiring/attempting to commit/advocating/abetting/advising/inciting or knowingly facilitating the commission of a terrorist act
- Punishment for organising camp to train terrorists or recruiting persons for committing terrorist acts
- Punishment for being a member of organisation involved in terrorist act
- Harbouring or concealing a terrorist
- Punishment for possessing proceeds of terrorist acts
- Powers of Police and Magistrate to combat such crime

Theft, ***para 1.50***

- Expanded definition of "theft" *vis-a-vis* IPC [Section 303(1) read with section 112(1) and section 2(*21*)]
- Prescribed punishment [section 303(2)]
- Community service as punishment for first-time convict if he returns value of stolen property or restores stolen property
- Snatching
- Mandatory Summary trial of offences of petty theft
- When offence of theft is punishable under this section and when punishable u/s 112
- Powers of Police and Magistrate to combat such crime

Theft by clerk or servant of property in possession of master, ***para 1.51***

- Mandatory Summary trial

Theft in a dwelling house, or means of transportation or place of worship, etc., ***para 1.52***

- Enlarged definition
- Mandatory Summary trial

- When offence of theft from vehicle, dwelling house or business premises is punishable under section 305 and when punishable u/s 112

Treason, acts endangering sovereignty, unity and integrity of India, ***para 1.53***

- Treason
- Act endangering sovereignty, unity and integrity of India

Trick theft, ***para 1.54***

- Trick theft
- When trick theft is punishable as theft under section 303(2) and when punishable u/s 112(2) as petty organised crime

Unnatural offences, ***para 1.55***

Weights and measures, offences relating to, ***para 1.56***

Woman, enticing or taking away or detaining with criminal intent a married woman, ***para 1.57***

- Woman under husband care or any other person

UNDERSTANDING OFFENCES AND PUNISHMENT UNDER BHARATIYA NYAYA SANHITA, 2023 (BNS)

AADHAAR CARD , FORGERY OF [SECTION 337 OF BNS/SECTION 466 OF IPC] [1.1]

Aadhaar Card

- Unlike section 466 of IPC, section 337 of BNS specifically makes it an offence to forge identity document issued by Government including Aadhaar card and Voter identity card.
- The offence is punishable with imprisonment of either description for a term which may extend to seven years, and shall also be liable to fine.

ABETMENT OUTSIDE INDIA FOR OFFENCE COMMITTED IN INDIA [SECTION 48 OF BNS] [NEW PROVISION] [1.2]

Abatement outside India

- Section 48 of BNS is a new provision
- Section 48 of BNS provides that a person abets an offence within the meaning of this Sanhita who, without and beyond India, abets the commission of any act in India which would constitute an offence if committed in India.
- Abetment by a person outside India has been made an offence under section 48 to allow prosecution of person located in foreign country.

ADULTERY [SECTION 497 OF IPC (OMITTED BY BNS)] [1.3]

Adultery

- Hitherto, adultery was a punishable offence under section 497 of IPC
- BNS has omitted the offence of adultery

BEGGARY [SECTION 143 OF BNS/SECTION 370 OF IPC] [1.4]

Beggary

- Beggary has been introduced as a form of exploitation for trafficking and made punishable under section 143 of the BNS. [*Explanation 1* to section 143(1) of BNS].
- The definition of exploitation in *Explanation 1* to section 370(1) of IPC did not cover beggary in its scope.

BLACK MARKETING OF CINEMA/MATCH TICKETS [SECTION 112 OF BNS] [NEW PROVISION] [1.5]

Black marketing of tickets

- Ticket resale is also known as ticket scalping or ticket touting. It is an act of reselling tickets for admission to events.
- Resale of Tickets through secondary sources may be for less or more than their face value depending on demand, which itself tends to vary as the event date approaches. When the supply of tickets for a given event available through authorized ticket sellers is depleted, the event is considered "sold out", generally increasing the market value for any tickets on offer through secondary sellers.
- Ticket scalping or ticket touting is commonly known as 'black marketing of tickets'.

Punishability of Ticket scalping or ticket touting was grey area under IPC

- Hitherto, the legality of secondary sale of tickets of concerts or movies or matches in India was not very clear-cut, and there was no specific law dealing with this issue. None of the sections of the IPC dealt with this. Hitherto, this was considered to be a legal grey area.

Unauthorised selling of tickets by a member of a group or gang is punishable as petty organised crime under BNS

- To plug this loophole and bring clarity in regard to legality of ticket scalping, BNS has brought unauthorised selling of tickets by a member of a group or gang within the ambit of new offence of "petty organised crime" under section 112 of BNS.
- Section 112(1) of BNS provides that if a member of a group or gang, either singly or jointly, commits unauthorised selling of tickets, he is said to commit the offence of petty organised crime. [Section 112(1) of BNS].
- Therefore, black marketing of cinema tickets by a member of a gang or a group is punishable as "petty organised crime".
- Whoever commits any petty organised crime shall be punished with imprisonment for a term which shall not be less than one year but which may extend to seven years, and shall also be liable to fine.[Section 112(2)]

Meaning of "unauthorised selling of tickets"

- The important point to note is that it is "unauthorized selling of tickets" which comes under petty organised crime. Whether ticket scalping or ticket resale is unauthorized or not depends upon the terms and conditions of the tickets themselves and any provisions of local laws in the States.

BREACH OF PEACE, INTENTIONAL INSULT WITH INTENT TO PROVOKE [SECTION 352 OF BNS/SECTION 504 OF IPC] [1.6]

Mandatory Summary trial

- Offence of insult with intent to provoke a breach of the peace under section 352 of BNS is now mandatorily to be tried summarily as per section 283(1)(*v*) of Bharatiya Nagarik Suraksha Sanhita, 2023 (BNSS). Under section 260 of Cr.PC, it was summarily triable by Magistrate at his discretion. Offences enumerated in section 283(1) of Bharatiya Nagarik Suraksha Sanhita, 2023 (BNSS) are mandatorily to be tried summarily by Magistrates.

CAUSING DEATH BY NEGLIGENCE [SECTION 106(1) OF BNS/ SECTION 304A OF IPC] [1.7]

Increased punishment

- Section 106(1) of BNS provides that whoever causes death of any person by doing any rash or negligent act not amounting to culpable homicide, shall be punished with imprisonment of either description for a term which may extend to five years (2 years under section 304A of IPC).
- The new law increases the punishment for causing death by negligence from a maximum of two years to a maximum of five years. This change reflects a stricter approach to cases of negligence resulting in death.
- *See* also **Hit and run cases** and also **Medical Practitioner causing death by his negligent act in medical procedure**.

CHEATING [SECTION 318 OF BNS/SECTIONS 415, 417, 418 AND 420 OF IPC] [1.8]

Prescribed punishment

- Punishment for cheating by way of imprisonment increased from 1 year (section 417 of IPC) to 3 years (under section 318(2) of BNS)
- Punishment by way of imprisonment for cheating a person whose interest the offender was bound to protect has been increased from 3 years (section 418 of IPC) to 5 years (under section 318(3) of BNS)

When offence of cheating is punishable under this section and when punishable u/s 112

- If offender committing cheating is a member of a gang or group, the offence of cheating is punishable under section 112 as petty organized crime.
- If he commits it as a lone wolf (operating by himself solo and not part of gang/group), it will be punishable under this section.

CHEATING

[Definition : Section 318(1)]

↓

If offender is part of a group or a gang	If offender is a lone wolf (sole operator not part of any group or gang)
↓	↓
Punishable as petty organised crime under section 112(2) of BNS [Non-compoundable offence]	Punishable under section 318(2)/318(3)/318(4) [offence under section 318(2) is compoundable u/s 359(1) of BNSS; offence u/s 318(3) and 318(4) are compoundable u/s 359(2) of BNSS]

CHILD [SECTION 2(*3*) OF BNS] [1.9]

Child

- ***Section 2(3) of BNS is a new provision*** **[NEW]**
- Section 2(*3*) of BNS defines 'child' to means any person below the age of 18 years

CHILD, HIRING, EMPLOYING OR ENGAGING TO COMMIT AN OFFENCE [SECTION 95 OF BNS] [1.10]

Hiring child to commit an offence

- ***Section 95 of BNS is a new provision*** **[NEW]**
- Section 95 of BNS provides that whoever hires, employs or engages any person below the age of eighteen years to commit an offence shall be punished for with imprisonment of either description or fine provided for that offence as if the offence has been committed by such person himself.
- Hiring, employing, engaging or using a child for sexual exploitation or pornography is covered within the meaning of this section.

CIVIL RECOVERY OF PROCEEDS OF CRIME AND DISTRIBUTION TO VICTIMS OF CRIME [SECTION 4 OF BNS AND SECTION 107 OF BNSS (NEW PROVISION)/SECTION 53 OF IPC] [1.11]

Civil recovery

- New provision of Civil recovery of proceeds of crime is *brahmastra* for Police and Magistrate to combat crimes [Section 107 of Bharatiya Nagarik Suraksha Sanhita (BNSS)] by seizing and attaching proceeds of crime and distribution to victims even during investigation without awaiting outcome of trial
- Section 107 is a radical new thinking that allows civil recovery of proceeds of crime unlike traditional model of confiscation of proceeds of crime after conviction of the offenders
- Police can apply for and Magistrate can attach and seize and effect civil recovery of proceeds of crime and distribute it to victims during investigation itself without awaiting trial outcome. [Section 107 of BNSS]
- Unclaimed proceeds of crime will be forfeited to Government (civil forfeiture of assets).
- For details, *see* **'Forfeiture of Property'**.

COIN, CURRENCY-NOTES, BANK NOTES AND GOVERNMENT STAMPS, OFFENCES RELATING TO - POSSESSION OF FORGED OR COUNTERFEIT COINS, GOVERNMENT STAMP, CURRENCY-NOTES OR BANK-NOTES [SECTION 180 OF BNS/SECTION 242 OF IPC] [1.12]

Possession of counterfeit currency

- Section 242 of IPC has been amended and introduced as section 180 in BNS to protect the public who are merely in possession of forged or counterfeit currency-notes or bank-notes etc. Under the amended law, mere possession of forged or counterfeit currency-notes or bank-notes etc. is not an offence.
- The amended law (section 180 of BNS) provides that in order to constitute an offence of possession of counterfeit currency note, it has to be accompanied by the intention to use the same as genuine.

COMMUNITY SERVICE [SECTION 4 OF BNS/SECTION 53 OF IPC/SECTION 23 OF BNSS] [1.13]

Community Service

- Section 53 of IPC provided for 5 types of punishments *viz.* (*1*) Death; (*2*) Imprisonment for life; (*3*) Imprisonment which is of two descriptions–rigorous and simple; (*4*) Forfeiture of property and (*5*) Fine. Section 4(*f*) of BNS has introduced a new 6th type of punishment - Community service
- To reduce the burden on jails, community service has been included in BNS as a punishment for the first time and it is being given legal status. [*PIB Press Release, dated 20-12-2023*]
- The term "community service" is not defined in BNS. However, it is defined by *Explanation* to section 23 of Bharatiya Nagarik Suraksha Sanhita (BNSS) to mean the work which the Court may order a convict to perform as a form of punishment that benefits the community, for which he shall not be entitled to any remuneration.

Offences for which punishment of community service can be awarded

- BNS prescribes Community Service as punishment for 6 petty offences
- Under BNS, Community service can be awarded as punishment in case of following offences:

Section	*Offence*
Section 202	Public servant unlawfully engaging in trade.
Section 209	Non-appearance in response to a proclamation under section 84 of Bharatiya Nagarik Suraksha Sanhita, 2023.
Section 226	Attempt to commit suicide to compel or restraint exercise of lawful power.
Proviso below section 303(2)	In cases of theft where the value of the stolen property is less than five thousand rupees, and a person is convicted for the first time, shall upon return of the value of property or restoration of the stolen property, shall be punished with community service.
Section 355	Misconduct in public by a drunken person.
Section 356	Defamation

COMMUNITY SERVICE/PAYMENT OF FINE, DEFAULT OF [SECTION 8 OF BNS/SECTIONS 63 TO 70 OF IPC] [1.14]

Community service

- IPC only provided for imprisonment in default of fine only. As there was no punishment of community service in IPC, there was also no imprisonment in default of community service in IPC.
- Consequent upon introduction of new punishment of community service [See section 4 of BNS] by the BNS, sub-sections (4) and (5) of section 8 of BNS provide for imposing imprisonment in default of community service.

Default in payment of fine or default of community service

- Under old law for default in payment of fine following punishment followed:
  - Fine not exceeding ₹ 50 - Imprisonment not exceeding 2 months
  - Fine not exceeding ₹ 100 - Imprisonment not exceeding 4 months
  - In any other case - Imprisonment not exceeding 6 months
- Under BNS for default in payment of fine or default of community service following punishment follows:
  - Fine not exceeding ₹ 5000 or community service - Imprisonment not exceeding 2 months
  - Fine not exceeding ₹ 10,000 or community service - Imprisonment not exceeding 4 months
  - In any other case - Imprisonment not exceeding 1 year

CONSTRUCTION, NEGLIGENT CONDUCT WITH RESPECT TO PULLING DOWN, REPAIRING OR CONSTRUCTING BUILDINGS, ETC. [SECTION 290 OF BNS/SECTION 288 OF IPC] [1.15]

Scope of provision

- The primary difference between section 288 of IPC and the section 290 of BNS is the expanded scope of the offence under the new law. While the old law specifically mentioned 'pulling down or repairing buildings', the new law also includes 'constructing buildings' within its scope. This means that individuals involved in construction activities must also take measures to guard against probable danger to human life

Prescribed fine

- Amount of fine increased five-fold from ₹ 1000 to ₹ 5000

COUNTERFEIT SEAL ETC., MAKING OR POSSESSING, WITH INTENT TO COMMIT FORGERY PUNISHABLE UNDER SECTION 338 [SECTION 341 OF BNS/SECTIONS 472 AND 473 OF IPC] [1.16]

Counterfeiting

- ***Sub-sections (3) and (4) of section 341 of BNS are new provisions.*** **[NEW]**
- They create new offences and provide for their punishments. There were no corresponding provisions in IPC.
- Section 341(3) of BNS provides that whoever possesses any seal, plate or other instrument knowing the same to be counterfeit, shall be punished with imprisonment of either description for a term which may extend to three years, and shall also be liable to fine.
- Section 341(4) of BNS provides that whoever fraudulently or dishonestly uses as genuine any seal, plate or other instrument knowing or having reason to believe the same to be counterfeit, shall be punished in the same manner as if he had made or counterfeited such seal, plate or other instrument.

DAMAGE TO GOVERNMENT PROPERTY [SECTION 324 OF BNS/ SECTIONS 425 TO 427 AND 440 OF IPC] [1.17]

Damage to Government property

- ***Sub-section (3) of section 324 is a new provision.*** There was no corresponding provision in IPC. It provides that whoever commits mischief and thereby causes loss or damage to any property including the property of Government or Local Authority shall be punished with imprisonment of either description for a term which may extend to one year, or with fine, or with both
- The threshold monetary limit for value of loss or damage caused by mischief is increased from ₹ 50 in section 427 of IPC to ₹ 20,000 (but less than ₹ 1,00,000) in section 324(4) of BNS
- Imprisonment is increased from 2 years under section 427 of IPC to 5 years under section 324(5) of BNS where loss or damage by mischief exceeds ₹ 1,00,000.

DEFAMATION [SECTION 356 OF BNS/SECTION 499 OF IPC] [1.18]

Any manner

- Section 356(1) of BNS provides that 'whoever .... publishes *in any manner*'. Words 'in any manner' were not there in section 499 of IPC

Community service

- Court can impose community service as a punishment instead of simple imprisonment or fine or both

DOCUMENT [SECTION 2(*8*) OF BNS/SECTION 29 OF IPC] [1.19]

- Section 2(*8*) of BNS provides that 'document' includes 'electronics and digital record'
- An electronic record on emails, server logs, documents on computers, laptop or smartphone, messages, websites, locational evidence and voice mail messages stored on digital devices are documents [*See* also section 2(*1*)(*c*) of Bharatiya Sakshya Adhiniyam, 2023 (BSA)]

DRUNKEN PERSON, MISCONDUCT IN PUBLIC BY [SECTION 355 OF BNS/SECTION 510 OF IPC] [1.20]

Community service

- Court can impose community service as a punishment instead of simple imprisonment of 24 hours or fine or both

FORFEITURE OF PROPERTY [SECTION 4 OF BNS AND SECTION 107 OF BNSS (NEW PROVISION)/SECTION 53 OF IPC] [1.21]

Forfeiture of property

- Forfeiture of property was a punishment u/s 53 of IPC. That position still continues u/s 4(*e*) of BNS.
- BNS does not specify the procedure for forfeiture of proceeds of crime nor what will be done with forfeited property. All this is specified in new provision of section 107 of BNSS

New provision of section 107 of BNSS provides that proceeds of crime will be distributed among victims and unclaimed amount will be forfeited to Govt.

- The new provision of section 107 of BNSS provides for attachment and forfeiture of property which are proceeds of crime and distribution of the proceeds among victims. Proceeds of crime unclaimed by victims shall be forfeited to Government.
- Above powers are exercisable by Police and Magistrate even during investigation. Dealing with proceeds of crime and giving relief to victims is not required to wait till conclusion of trial.

Attachment of property derived or obtained, directly or indirectly, as a result of a criminal activity or from the commission of any offence

- Where a police officer making an investigation has reason to believe
- that any property is derived or obtained, directly or indirectly, as a result of a criminal activity or from the commission of any offence,
- he may,
- with the approval of the Superintendent of Police or Commissioner of Police,
- make an application to the Court or the Judicial Magistrate exercising jurisdiction to take cognizance of the offence or commit for trial or try the case, for the attachment of such property. [Section 107(1)]

Procedure for attachment of properties which are proceeds of crime

ISSUE OF SHOW CAUSE NOTICE

- If the Court or the Judicial Magistrate has reasons to believe, whether before or after taking evidence, that all or any of such properties are proceeds of crime, the Court or the Magistrate may issue a notice upon such person
- Notice shall call upon him to show cause within a period of fourteen days as to why an order of attachment shall not be made. [Section 107(2)]
- Where the notice issued to any person under sub-section (2) specifies any property as being held by any other person on behalf of such person, a copy of the notice shall also be served upon such other person. [Section 107(3)]

ORDER OF ATTACHMENT IN RESPECT OF PROPERTIES FOUND TO BE PROCEEDS OF TIME

- The Court or the Judicial Magistrate may,
- after considering the explanation, if any, to the show-cause notice issued under sub-section (2) and the material fact available before

such Court or Magistrate and

- after giving a reasonable opportunity of being heard to such person or persons,
- may pass an order of attachment, in respect of those properties which are found to be the proceeds of crime.

EX PARTE ORDER OF ATTACHMENT IF SUCH PERSON DOES NOT APPEAR BEFORE COURT/MAGISTRATE WITHIN 14 DAYS SPECIFIED IN SCN

- If such person does not appear before the Court or the Magistrate or represent his case before the Court or Judicial Magistrate within a period of fourteen days specified in the show-cause notice, the Court or the Judicial Magistrate may proceed to pass the *ex parte* order. [Section 107(4)]

INTERIM *EX PARTE* ORDER OF ATTACHMENT WITHOUT ISSUING SCN

- Notwithstanding anything contained in sub-section (2),
- if the Court or the Judicial Magistrate is of the opinion that issuance of notice under the said sub-section would defeat the object of attachment or seizure,
- the Court or Judicial Magistrate may by an interim order passed *ex parte* direct attachment or seizure of such property, and
- such order shall remain in force till an order under sub-section (6) is passed. [Section 107(5)]

Rateable distribution of attached/seized among victims of crime if attached/seized properties found to be proceeds of crime

- If the Court or the Judicial Magistrate finds the attached or seized properties to be the proceeds of crime, the Court or the Judicial Magistrate shall by order direct the District Magistrate to rateably distribute such proceeds of crime to the persons who are affected by such crime.[Section 107(6)]
- On receipt of an order passed under sub-section (6), the District Magistrate shall, within a period of sixty days distribute the proceeds of crime either by himself or authorise any officer subordinate to him to effect such distribution. [Section 107(7)]

Proceeds of crime to be forfeited to government if no claimants to receive such proceeds

- If there are no claimants to receive such proceeds or no claimant is ascertainable or there is any surplus after satisfying the claimants, such proceeds of crime shall stand forfeited to the Government. [Section 107(8)]

FORGERY OF VOTER IDENTITY CARD [SECTION 337 OF BNS/ SECTION 466 OF IPC] [1.22]

Voter-Id Card

- Unlike section 466 of IPC, section 337 of BNS specifically makes it an offence to forge identity document issued by Government including Aadhaar card and Voter identity card.
- The offence is punishable with imprisonment of either description for a term which may extend to seven years, and shall also be liable to fine.

GENDER [SECTION 2(*10*) OF BNS/SECTION 8 OF IPC] [1.23]

Transgender recognised as gender and defined

- The definition of "gender" in section 8 of IPC recognizes only male and female genders. The new definition of "gender" in section 2(*10*) of BNS recognizes "transgender" in addition to genders of "male" and "female".

GRIEVOUS HURT, VOLUNTARILY CAUSING [SECTION 117 OF BNS/SECTIONS 322 AND 325 OF IPC] [1.24]

Causing permanent disability

- ***Section 117(3) and (4) are new provision*** [NEW]
- Section 117(3) of BNS provides that whoever commits an offence under sub-section (1) of section 117 and in the course of such commission causes any hurt to a person which causes that person to be in permanent disability or in persistent vegetative state, shall be punished with rigorous imprisonment for a term which shall not be less than ten years but which may extend to imprisonment for life, which shall mean imprisonment for the remainder of that person's natural life.

Mob lynching - Grievous hurt

- Section 117(4) of BNS provides that when a group of five or more persons acting in concert, causes grievous hurt to a person on the ground of his race, caste or community, sex, place of birth, language, personal belief or any other similar ground, each member of such group shall be guilty of the offence of causing grievous hurt, and shall be punished with imprisonment of either description for a term which may extend to seven years, and shall also be liable to fine.

HIT AND RUN CASES [SECTION 106(2)* OF BNS/SECTION 304A OF IPC] [1.25]

Increased punishment

- Section 106(1) of BNS provides that whoever causes death of any person by doing any rash or negligent act not amounting to culpable homicide, shall be punished with imprisonment of either description for a term which may extend to five years.
- The new law increases the punishment for causing death by negligence from a maximum of two years (under section 304A of IPC) to a maximum of five years. This change reflects a stricter approach to cases of negligence resulting in death.

Offender escaping or failing to report **[NEW]**

- Section 106(2) introduces an additional provision in sub-section (2) to section 106 of BNS, which addresses situations where the offender escapes from the scene of the incident without reporting it to a police officer or Magistrate after the incident. In such cases, the punishment is very severe, with a maximum term of imprisonment of ten years with fine. [Section 106(2)]
- As the instances of hit and run cases are on the rise, a new provision under section 106(2) of BNS has been made. Currently hit and run cases resulting in death due to reckless and negligent driving are registered u/s 304A of IPC, with maximum penalty of two years of imprisonment. As per Delhi Road Crash Report of 2021, there were 555 cases (46.01% of total cases) where the registration number of vehicles involved in crime were unknown, signifying hit and run cases. The Supreme Court had in several cases observed on the inadequacy of law in view of increased vehicular accident. To address this issue, the new provision has been introduced under clause 106(2), which was long overdue.
- Section 106(2) has been introduced to cover the hit and run accidents and to ensure reporting of accident immediately. This has been introduced with an aim to save the victim within the critical 'Golden Hour', a term introduced in the Motor Vehicles Act, 1988 in the year 2019.
- Punishment under section 106(2) is not attracted merely by virtue of driver escaping from the scene after the incident to escape the wrath of bystanders who might mob-lynch him. *Offence is*

***Notification No. S.O. 850(E), dated 23-2-2024** - In exercise of the powers conferred by sub-section (2) of section 1 of the Bharatiya Nyaya Sanhita, 2023 (45 of 2023), the Central Government hereby appoints the 1st day of July, 2024 as the date on which the provisions of the said Sanhita, except the provision of sub-section (2) of section 106, shall come into force.

committed only if escape from scene is coupled with non-reporting by him to Police or Magistrate soon after the incident.

KIDNAPPING OR MAIMING A CHILD FOR PURPOSE OF BEGGING [SECTIONS 111 AND 139 OF BNS/ SECTION 363A OF IPC] [1.26]

Prescribed punishment

- Punishment by way of imprisonment for kidnapping or obtaining custody of a child so that it may be used or employed for begging, has been enhanced from imprisonment of either description of 10 years to rigorous imprisonment for a term which shall not be less than ten years but which may extend to imprisonment for life
- Punishment by way of imprisonment for maiming a child for purposes of begging has been enhanced from imprisonment for life to imprisonment which shall not be less than twenty years, but which may extend to life

Child

- For the word 'minor', word 'child' is used. Child may be a male child or female child

LIFE IMPRISONMENT [SECTION 4 OF BNS/SECTION 53 OF IPC] [1.27]

Life imprisonment

- The punishment of imprisonment for life has been clearly defined as imprisonment for remainder of a person's natural life

MEDICAL PRACTITIONER CAUSING DEATH BY HIS NEGLIGENT ACT IN MEDICAL PROCEDURE[SECTION 106 OF BNS/ SECTION 304A OF IPC] [1.28]

Death caused by Medical practitioner's negligence in performing medical procedure

- In case of registered medical practitioner if negligent act is done by a registered medical practitioner while performing medical procedure, he shall be punished with imprisonment of either description for a term which may extend to two years, and shall also be liable to fine.

Definition of "Registered Medical Practitioner"

- For the purposes of this sub-section, "registered medical practitioner" means a medical practitioner who possesses any medical qualification recognised under the National Medical Commission Act, 2019 (30 of 2019) and whose name has been entered in the National Medical Register or a State Medical Register under that Act.

MOB LYNCHING - DEATH [SECTION 103(2) OF BNS][NEW PROVISION] [1.29]

Mob Lynching (Death)

- ***Section 103(2) of BNS is a new provision*** [NEW]
- Section 103(2) of BNS provides that when a group of five or more persons acting in concert commits murder on the ground of race, caste or community, sex, place of birth, language, personal belief or any other ground each member of such group shall be punished with death or with imprisonment for life, and shall also be liable to fine.

MOB LYNCHING (HURT OR GRIEVOUS HURT) [SECTION 117(4) OF BNS] [1.30]

Mob lynching (hurt/grievous hurt)

- ***Section 117(4) of BNS is a new provision*** **[NEW]**
- Section 117(4) of BNS provides that when a group of five or more persons acting in concert, causes grievous hurt to a person on the ground of his race, caste or community, sex, place of birth, language, personal belief or any other similar ground, each member of such group shall be guilty of the offence of causing grievous hurt, and shall be punished with imprisonment of either description for a term which may extend to seven years, and shall also be liable to fine.

MONTH AND YEAR [SECTION 2(20) OF BNS/SECTION 49 OF IPC] [1.31]

Reference to British calendar replaced with reference to Gregorian calendar

- Section 49 of IPC required year or month to be reckoned as per

British calendar while section 2(*20*) of BNS requires year or month to be reckoned as per the Gregorian calendar

MOVABLE PROPERTY [SECTION 2(*21*) OF BNS/SECTION 22 OF IPC] [1.32]

Scope of "Movable property" in section 2(21) not limited to property in corporeal form, unlike the definition in section 22

- Section 2(*21*) of BNS omits the word "are intended to include corporeal" before the word "property" which was there in the definition of movable property in section 22 of IPC
- Therefore, movable property includes property of every description other than immovable property whether such property is in corporeal (tangible physical) form or not.

Impact of changes in definition of movable property

- Definition of movable property in BNS will include intangible assets such as patents, copyrights etc. It will also include actionable claims and data.
- In view of expanded definition of movable property, "theft" (See section 303) will include theft of intangible assets, theft of data, theft of credit card data through card skimming, online theft through hacking bank accounts or cloning the mobile, identity theft, etc.
- It appears that piracy of products, infringing copyrights, etc., shall now be covered under 'theft' (See section 303)

NATIONAL INTEGRATION, IMPUTATIONS, ASSERTIONS PREJUDICIAL TO [SECTION 197 OF BNS/SECTION 153B OF IPC] [1.33]

Electronic communication

- Under section 197 of BNS, 'electronic communication' is added as one of the mode of spreading specified activities. This was not the case in section 153B of IPC.

False information

- Section 197(1)(*d*) of BNS additionally cover activity of making or publishing false or misleading information jeopardising the sovereignty, unity and integrity or security of India. [NEW]

ORGANISED CRIME [SECTION 111 OF BNS] [NEW PROVISION] [1.34]

Organised Crime

- Hitherto, IPC does not have any section dealing with Organised crime by Organised crime syndicates/gangs. Organised Crime is dealt with by State laws like Maharashtra Control of Organised Crime Act,1999 (MCOCA,1999)

  The following are the ingredients of "Organised crime":

- *Continuing unlawful activity:* It is any continuing unlawful activity including:
  - kidnapping,
  - robbery,
  - vehicle theft,
  - extortion,
  - land grabbing,
  - contract killing,
  - economic offence,
  - cyber-crimes*,

---

* - Cyber crimes includes
    - Cyber Bullying/Stalking/Sexting
    - E-Mail Hacking
    - E-Mail Phishing
    - Fake/Impersonating Profile
    - Impersonating Email
    - Online Job Fraud
    - Online Matrimonial Fraud
    - Profile Hacking
    - Online Financial Fraud
    - Business Email Takeover
    - Debit/Credit Card Fraud
    - E-Wallet Related Fraud
    - Fraud Call/Vishing
    - Internet banking Related Fraud
    - SIM Swap Fraud
  - Ransomware
  - Hacking
  - Cryptocurrency Related Crime
  - Online Trafficking
  - Online Gambling
  - Any Other Cyber Crime

- trafficking in persons, drugs, weapons or illicit goods or services,
- human trafficking for prostitution or ransom

- *Activity carried on by member/members of organised crime syndicate:* Such activity is carried on by any person or a group of persons acting in concert, singly or jointly, either as a member of an organised crime syndicate or on behalf of such syndicate,
- *Unlawful means*: Such activity is carried on by use of violence, threat of violence, intimidation, coercion, or by any other unlawful means
- *Aim is to obtain a benefit:* Such activity is carried on to obtain direct or indirect, material benefit including a financial benefit,

Definition of "Continuing unlawful activity" [Clause *(ii)* of *Explanation* below Section 111(1)]

The definition of "Continuing unlawful activity" has two limbs as under:

(*A*) *First limb :* The term "continuing unlawful activity" means:

- an activity prohibited by law,
- which is a cognizable offence punishable with imprisonment of 3 years or more
- undertaken by any person, either singly or jointly, as a member of an organised crime syndicate or on behalf of such syndicate
- in respect of which more than one charge-sheets have been filed before a competent court within the preceding period of ten years and
- that court has taken cognizance of such offence.

(*B*) *Second limb (inclusive limb) :* The term "continuing unlawful activity" includes economic offence whether or not the ingredients in (*A*) above are satisfied or not. In other words, economic offence would be "Continuing unlawful activity" irrespective of whether or not it is a cognizable offence punishable with imprisonment of 3 years or more, whether or not in respect of it more than one charge-sheets have been filed before a competent court within the preceding period of ten years and whether or not court has taken cognizance of the offence.

Definition of "Economic offence" [Clause *(iii)* of *Explanation* below Section 111(1)]

"Economic offences" includes the following offences committed for obtaining the monetary benefits in any form:

- criminal breach of trust,

- forgery,
- counterfeiting of currency-notes, bank-notes and Government Stamps,
- *hawala* transaction,
- mass-marketing fraud or
- running any scheme to defraud several persons or
- doing any act in any manner with a view to defraud any bank or financial institution or any other institution

The offences enumerated as above shall be regarded as "economic offences" if committed for obtaining the monetary benefits in any form. The above definition of "economic offence" is apparently an inclusive one. It appears that any offence committed for obtaining monetary benefits in any form will be an economic offence. However, that does not appear to be the intention if one takes into account section 112. "Petty organised crime" as defined in section 112 shall not be economic offences punishable under this section though those may be committed for obtaining monetary benefits in any form. Petty organised crime is punishable under section 112. Therefore, it appears that the definition of economic offences in *Explanation (iii)* to section 111(1) is exhaustive.

Continuing unlawful activity/Economic offence/Other unlawful activity

Unlawful activities specifically enumerated in section 111(1) which are per se *'continuing unlawful activity'*	*Economic offences which are* per se *'continuing unlawful activity'*	*Other unlawful activities, when 'continuing unlawful activity'*
(1)	*(2)*	*(3)*
◆ contract killing, ◆ cyber-crimes, ◆ economic offence, ◆ extortion, ◆ human trafficking for prostitution or ransom ◆ kidnapping, ◆ land grabbing, ◆ robbery,	"Economic offences" includes the following offences committed for obtaining the monetary benefits in any form: ◆ act done in any manner with a view to defraud any bank or financial institution or any other institution ◆ counterfeiting of currency-notes, bank-	Any other unlawful activity (activity prohibited by law) other than those in Columns (1) and (2): Any other unlawful activity is continuing unlawful activity if all the following conditions are satisfied: ◆ an activity prohibited by law,

Unlawful activities specifically enumerated in section 111(1) which are per se *'continuing unlawful activity'*	*Economic offences which are* per se *'continuing unlawful activity'*	*Other unlawful activities, when 'continuing unlawful activity'*
(1)	*(2)*	*(3)*
◆ trafficking in persons, drugs, weapons or illicit goods or services, ◆ vehicle theft All the above enumerated activities are Continuing unlawful activities *per se* irrespective of whether 2 or more charge-sheets have been filed before a competent Court within the preceding period of 10 years and whether the Court has taken cognizance of such offence. The above are Continuing unlawful activities *per se* so long as these are undertaken by any person, either singly or jointly, as a member of an organised crime syndicate (group of 2 or more persons) or on behalf of such syndicate	notes and Government Stamps, ◆ criminal breach of trust; ◆ forgery, ◆ *hawala* transaction, ◆ mass-marketing fraud or ◆ running any scheme to defraud several persons Economic offences are Continuing unlawful activities *per se* irrespective of whether these are cognizable offences punishable with imprisonment of 3 years or more or whether or not 2 or more charge-sheets have been filed before a competent Court within the preceding period of 10 years or whether the Court has taken cognizance of such offence. The above are continuing unlawful activities *per se* so long as these are undertaken by any person, either singly or jointly, as a member of an organised crime syndicate(group of 2 or more persons) or on behalf of such syndicate.	◆ which is a cognizable offence punishable with imprisonment of 3 years or more ◆ undertaken by any person, either singly or jointly, as a member of an organised crime syndicate or on behalf of such syndicate ◆ in respect of which more than one charge-sheets have been filed before a competent court within the preceding period of ten years and ◆ that court has taken cognizance of such offence.

New definition of "Organised crime syndicate" [Clause *(i)* of *Explanation* below Section 111(1)]

"Organised crime syndicate" means a group of three or more persons who, acting either singly or jointly, as a syndicate or gang indulge in any continuing unlawful activity

Punishment for committing organized crime [Section 111(2)]

- Whoever commits organised crime shall,—

  (*a*) if such offence has resulted in the death of any person, be punished with death or imprisonment for life, and shall also be liable to fine which shall not be less than ten lakh rupees;

  (*b*) in any other case, be punished with imprisonment for a term which shall not be less than five years but which may extend to imprisonment for life, and shall also be liable to fine which shall not be less than five lakh rupees.

Punishment for abetment of, attempt to commit, or facilitating organized crime or engaging in activity preparatory to organized crime [Section 111(3)]

- Whoever,
- abets, attempts, conspires or knowingly facilitates the commission of an organised crime, or
- otherwise engages in any act preparatory to an organised crime,
- shall be punished with imprisonment for a term which shall not be less than five years but which may extend to imprisonment for life, and shall also be liable to fine which shall not be less than rupees five lakhs.

Punishment for being a member of an organized crime syndicate [Section 111(4)]

- Any person who is a member of an organised crime syndicate shall be punished with imprisonment for a term which shall not be less than five years but which may extend to imprisonment for life, and shall also be liable to fine which shall not be less than five lakh rupees.

Punishment for intentionally harbouring or concealing any person who has committed the offence of an organised crime [Section 111(5)]

- Whoever, intentionally, harbours or conceals any person who has committed the offence of an organised crime shall be punished with imprisonment for a term which shall not be less than three years but which may extend to imprisonment for life, and shall also be liable to fine which shall not be less than five lakh rupees.

This provision shall not apply to any case in which the harbour or concealment is by the spouse of the offender.

Punishment for possession of any property derived or obtained from the commission of an organised crime or proceeds of any organised crime or which has been acquired through the organised crime [Section 111(6)]

- Whoever possesses any property derived or obtained from the commission of an organised crime or proceeds of any organised crime or which has been acquired through the organised crime, shall be punishable with imprisonment for a term which shall not be less than three years but which may extend to imprisonment for life and shall also be liable to fine which shall not be less than two lakh rupees.

Punishment for person in possession of any property on behalf of a member of an organized crime syndicate which he cannot satisfactorily account for [Section 111(7)]

- If any person on behalf of a member of an organised crime syndicate is, or at any time has been in possession of movable or immovable property which he cannot satisfactorily account for, shall be punishable with imprisonment for a term which shall not be less than three years but which may extend to imprisonment for ten years and shall also be liable to fine which shall not be less than one lakh rupees.

ORGANISED CRIME, PETTY [SECTION 112 OF BNS] [1.35]

Definition of "petty organized crime" [Section 112(2)]

- ***Section 112 of BNS is a new provision*** **[NEW]**
- Whoever, being a member of a group or gang, either singly or jointly, commits
  - any act of theft,
  - snatching,
  - cheating,
  - unauthorised selling of tickets,
  - unauthorised betting or gambling,

- selling of public examination question papers,
- or any other similar criminal act,

is said to commit petty organised crime.

Scope of the term "theft" [*Explanation* to section 112(1)]

For the purposes of this sub-section "theft" includes

- trick theft,
- theft from vehicle, dwelling house or business premises,
- cargo theft,
- pick pocketing,
- theft through card skimming,
- shoplifting and
- theft of Automated Teller Machine.

The terms "trick theft", "card skimming", "shoplifting", "pick pocketing" etc., are not defined in BNS. These terms will have to be understood as per their ordinary popular connotation.

Punishment for petty organized crime

- Whoever commits any petty organised crime shall be punished with imprisonment for a term which shall not be less than one year but which may extend to seven years, and shall also be liable to fine.

When offence of theft is punishable under this section and when punishable u/s 303 of BNS

- If offender committing "theft" is a member of a gang or group, offence is punishable under this section.
- If he commits it as a lone wolf (operating by himself solo and not part of gang/group), it will be punishable u/s 303

When offence of snatching is punishable under this section and when punishable u/s 304 of BNS

- If offender committing "snatching"(chain snatching, mobile snatching etc.) is a member of a gang or group, the offence of snatching is punishable under this section.
- If he commits it as a lone wolf (operating by himself solo and not part of gang/group), it will be punishable u/s 304 of BNS

When offence of cheating is punishable under this section and when punishable u/s 318

- If offender committing cheating is a member of a gang or group, the offence of cheating is punishable under this section.

- If he commits it as a lone wolf (operating by himself solo and not part of gang/group), it will be punishable u/s 318 of BNS

When offence of theft from vehicle, dwelling house or business premises is punishable under this section and when punishable u/s 305

- If offender committing the offence is a member of a gang or group, the offence is punishable under this section.
- If he commits it as a lone wolf (operating by himself solo and not part of gang/group), it will be punishable u/s 305

PROCLAIMED OFFENDER, NON-APPEARANCE IN RESPONSE TO A PROCLAMATION UNDER SECTION 84 OF BNSS, 2023 [SECTION 209 OF BNS/SECTION 174A OF IPC] [1.36]

Community service

- Judge trying the case is given an option to award sentence of community service for the offence of non-appearance in response to proclamation instead of imprisonment or fine or both

Scope of "proclaimed offenders" expanded by section 84 of BNSS

- BNSS expands the category of "proclaimed offenders" to include offences punishable with imprisonment of 10 years or more, life imprisonment, or the death penalty.

Joint Trial

- New *Explanation II* is added in section 24 of Bharatiya Sakshya Adhiniyam, 2023 so as to clarify that "A trial of more persons than one held in the absence of the accused who has absconded or who fails to comply with a proclamation issued under section 84 of the Bharatiya Nagarik Suraksha Sanhita, 2023 shall be deemed to be a joint trial for the purpose of this section."

PROMOTING ENMITY BETWEEN DIFFERENT GROUPS ON GROUNDS OF RELIGION, RACE, PLACE OF BIRTH, RESIDENCY, LANGUAGE, ETC., AND DOING ACTS PREJUDICIAL TO MAINTENANCE OF HARMONY [SECTION 196 OF BNS/SECTION 153A OF IPC] [1.37]

Electronic communication

- Under section 196 of BNS, 'electronic communication' is added as one of the mode of spreading disharmony, etc.

- The provisions relating to 'promoting of enmity between groups on the ground of religion, race, place of birth, language, etc. and doing acts prejudicial to maintenance of harmony' (section 153A of IPC) have been amended so as to cover offences committed through electronic communication - along with other means.

PUBLIC SERVANT, ASSAULTING OR OBSTRUCTING WHEN SUPPRESSING RIOT, ETC. [SECTION 195(1) OF BNS/SECTION 152 OF IPC] [1.38]

Scope of provisions

- The existing section 152 in IPC regarding 'assaulting or obstructing public servant when suppressing riot, etc.' has been divided into 2 parts and included in section 195 of the new law (BNS) - one for the offence of assault or obstruction of public servant and the other for threatening to assault or attempt to obstruct having different punishments and fine.

Prescribed punishment

- In cases where the offender actually assaults or obstructs a public servant or uses criminal force on a public servant in the described situations, the punishment includes imprisonment of either description for a term that may extend to three years, similar to the old law. However, the new law adds a significant change in the form of a minimum fine requirement. Offenders found guilty under section 195(1) of BNS shall be fined, and the fine shall not be less than ₹ 25,000
- In cases where the offender threatens to assault or attempts to obstruct a public servant or threatens or attempts to use criminal force on a public servant in the described situations, the punishment includes imprisonment of a term that may extend to one year. A fine may also be imposed under this sub-section **[NEW]**

PUBLIC SERVANT UNLAWFULLY ENGAGING IN TRADE [SECTION 202 OF BNS/SECTION 168 OF IPC] [1.39]

Community Service

- Judge trying the case is given an option to award sentence of community service for the offence instead of imprisonment or fine or both (section 202 of BNS). This option was not there in section 168 of IPC

PUBLISHING FALSE OR MISLEADING INFORMATION TO JEOPARDIZE SOVEREIGNTY UNITY AND INTEGRITY OR SECURITY OF INDIA [SECTION 197 OF BNS/SECTION 153B OF IPC] [1.40]

Electronic communication

- Under section 197 of BNS, 'electronic communication' is added as one of the mode of spreading specified activities. This was not the case under section 153B of IPC

False information

- Section 197(1)(*d*) of BNS additionally cover activity of 'making or publishing false or misleading information jeopardising the sovereignty, unity and integrity or security of India. [NEW]

PUNISHMENT, LIMIT OF, OF OFFENCE MADE OF SEVERAL OFFENCES [SECTION 9 OF BNS & SECTION 25 OF BNSS/SECTION 71 OF IPC & SECTION 31 OF CR.PC] [1.41]

Court to order punishments to run consecutively or concurrently after considering the gravity of the offences

- Section 31 of Cr.PC provided that when a person is convicted at one trial of two or more offences, the Court may sentence him for such offences to the several punishments prescribed therefor which such Court is competent to inflict. Section 31 further provided that such punishments when consisting of imprisonment to commence the one after the expiration of the other in such order as the Court may direct, unless the Court directs that such punishments shall run concurrently.
- Section 25 of BNSS provides that when a person is convicted at one trial of two or more offences, the Court may, subject to the provisions of section 9 of BNS, sentence him for such offences to the several punishments prescribed therefor which such Court is competent to inflict. Section 25 requires the Court to clearly order such punishments to run consecutively or concurrently after considering the gravity of offences.

RAPE [SECTIONS 63 TO 65 OF BNS/SECTIONS 375, 376 & 376AB OF IPC] [1.42]

Age of Consent by wife

- Exception 2 to section 63 of BNS provides that sexual intercourse or sexual acts by a man with his own wife, the wife not being under 18 years of age, is not rape. Under section 375 of IPC the age limit was 15 years.

Age of Consent of woman not being wife

- Clause (*i*) of section 64(2) of BNS provides for 'commits rape, on a woman incapable of giving consent'. Section 376(2)(*i*) of IPC provided for 'commits rape on woman when she is under 16 years of age'.

Offence of rape of under-aged women not capable of giving consent

- Section 65 of BNS combines both age categories (under 12 and under 16) into a single section, simplifying the legal framework.

Online FIR may be filed in respect of cognizable offence

- Section 173 of BNSS provides that every information relating to the commission of a cognizable offence, irrespective of the area where the offence is committed, may be given by electronic communication to the officer in charge of a Police station. In other words, section 173 allows for online "zero FIR" to be filed for offence of rape. Cr.PC contained no such enabling provision.

Recording of victim's statement by through any audio-video electronic means including mobile phone

- Third proviso to section 176(1) of BNSS permits recording of rape victim's statement through any audio-video electronic means including mobile phone.

RAPE, GANG [SECTION 70(2) OF BNS/SECTIONS 376DA AND 376DB OF IPC] [1.43]

Death penalty for gang rape of woman under 18 years of age

- Death sentence was provided under section 376DB of IPC for gang rape of woman under 12 years of age. No death penalty was provided for gang rape of woman aged below 16 but above

12 in section 376DA. Now, section 70(2) of BNS provides death penalty for gang rape of woman under 18 years of age.

Online FIR may be filed in respect of cognizable offence

- Section 173 of BNSS provides that every information relating to the commission of a cognizable offence, irrespective of the area where the offence is committed, may be given by electronic communication to the officer in charge of a Police station. In other words, section 173 allows for online "zero FIR" to be filed for offence of rape. Cr.PC contained no such enabling provision.

Recording of victim's statement by through any audio-video electronic means including mobile phone

- Third proviso to section 176(1) of BNSS permits recording of rape victim's statement through any audio-video electronic means including mobile phone.

SENTENCE, COMMUTATION OF [SECTION 5 OF BNS/SECTIONS 54 AND 55 OF IPC] [1.44]

Changes in commutation provisions : Section 433 of Cr.PC vis-a-vis section 474 of Bharatiya Nagarik Suraksha Sanhita, 2023 (BNSS)

- The comparison between section 433 of Cr.PC and section 474 of BNSS is tabulated below:

Sentence	*What the sentence in Col. (1) may be commuted for by appropriate govt. under section 433 of Cr.PC*	*What the sentence in Col. (1) may be commuted for by appropriate govt. under section 474 of BNSS*
(1)	*(2)*	*(3)*
Sentence of death	Appropriate Government may commute a death sentence for any other punishment provided by the Indian Penal Code	Death sentence may be commuted for imprisonment for life
Sentence of imprisonment for life	Sentence may be commuted for imprisonment for a term not exceeding fourteen years or for fine;	Sentence may be commuted for imprisonment for a term not less than 7 years

Sentence	*What the sentence in Col. (1) may be commuted for by appropriate govt. under section 433 of Cr.PC*	*What the sentence in Col. (1) may be commuted for by appropriate govt. under section 474 of BNSS*
(1)	*(2)*	*(3)*
A sentence for imprisonment for seven years or more	—	Sentence may be commuted for imprisonment for a term not less than 3 years
Sentence of rigorous imprisonment	Sentence may be commuted for simple imprisonment for any term to which that person might have been sentenced, or for fine;	Sentence may be commuted for simple imprisonment for any term to which that person might have been sentenced
Sentence of simple imprisonment	Sentence may be commuted for fine	—
Sentence for imprisonment for less than seven years	—	Sentence may be commuted for fine

SEXUAL INTERCOURSE BY EMPLOYING DECEITFUL MEANS [SECTION 69 OF BNS] [NEW PROVISION] [1.45]

- ***Section 69 of BNS is a new provision*** **[NEW]**
- *Offence punishable u/s 69* : Whoever, by deceitful means or making by promise to marry a woman without any intention of fulfilling the same, and has sexual intercourse with her, such sexual intercourse not amounting to the offence of rape.
- *"Deceitful means"* shall include the false promise of employment or promotion, inducement or marrying after suppressing identity.
- *Punishment* : Offender shall be punished with imprisonment of either description for a term which may extend to ten years and shall also be liable to fine.

SNATCHING [SECTIONS 304 AND 112 OF BNS/SECTIONS 379 AND 392 OF IPC] [1.46]

Definition of Snatching

- Theft is "snatching" if, in order to commit theft, the offender suddenly or quickly or forcibly seizes or secures or grabs or takes away from any person or from his possession any movable property [Section 304(1)]

Punishment for snatching

- Whoever commits snatching, shall be punished with imprisonment of either description for a term which may extend to three years, and shall also be liable to fine [Section 304(2)]

Snatching is petty organised crime if committed by a member of a group or a gang, either singly or jointly.

- Whoever, being a member of a group or gang, either singly or jointly, commits
  - any act of theft,
  - snatching,
  - cheating,
  - unauthorised selling of tickets,
  - unauthorised betting or gambling,
  - selling of public examination question papers
  - or any other similar criminal act,

  is said to commit petty organised crime.

Punishment for petty organized crime

- Whoever commits any petty organised crime shall be punished with imprisonment for a term which shall not be less than one year but which may extend to seven years, and shall also be liable to fine.

When offence of snatching is punishable under section 304(2) and when punishable u/s 112(2)

- If offender commits snatching as a lone wolf (operating by himself solo and not part of gang/group), it will be punishable under this section.
- If offender committing "snatching" (chain snatching, mobile snatching etc.) is a member of a gang or group, the offence of snatching is punishable under section 112 as petty organized crime.

Distinction between theft and snatching

The distinction between theft and snatching is summarised as under in the table below:

Sr. No.	*Points of comparison*	*Theft*	*Snatching*
(*a*)	Section of BNS under which punishable	303(2) (if offender not part of a group/gang)/ 112(2) (if offender part of a group/gang)	304(2) (if offender not part of a group/gang)/112(2) (if offender part of a group/ gang)
(*b*)	Definition	Section 303(1)/*Explanation* below section 112(1) read with section 2(21)	Section 304(1)
(*c*)	Scope of the term	Theft is a much wider term than snatching. Theft would cover theft of all kinds of movable property whether corporeal or non-corporeal. Theft would cover theft of intangible assets as also theft of data/theft of identity.	Snatching involves theft. However, every theft does not amount to snatching. A theft amounts to snatching when it satisfies the definition of theft under section 303(1) and the offender suddenly or quickly or forcibly seizes or secures or grabs or takes away from any person or from his possession any movable property. Further, theft can be of tangible movable property as well intangible assets while snatching can be only of tangible movable property.
(*d*)	Leniency where offence is by first time offender and value of stolen property is not much	In cases of theft where the value of the stolen property is less than five thousand rupees, and a person is convicted for the first time, shall upon return of the value of property or restoration of the stolen property, shall be punished with community service	No leniency in case of snatching even if first-time offender and value of stolen property is petty amount.

Sr. No.	*Points of comparison*	*Theft*	*Snatching*
(*e*)	Whether offence is summarily triable	Where the value of the property stolen does not exceed ₹ 20000, offence of theft under section 303(2) of BNS **shall** be tried in a summary way by any Chief Judicial Magistrate or Magistrate of the first class. Thus, summary trial is compulsory for petty thefts	The Magistrate ***may, after giving the accused a reasonable opportunity of being heard, for reasons to be recorded in writing***, try in a summary way all or any of the offences not punishable with death or imprisonment for life or imprisonment for a term exceeding three years. [Section 283(2) of BNSS]. It is discretionary for Magistrate to try or not to try snatching in a summary way.
(*f*)	Punishment	Imprisonment of either description for a term which may extend to three years, or with fine, or with both	Imprisonment of either description for a term which may extend to three years, and shall also be liable to fine.
(*g*)	Punishment for repeat offence	In case of second or subsequent conviction of any person under this section, he shall be punished with rigorous imprisonment for a term which shall not be less than one year but which may extend to five years and with fine:	—
(*h*)	Compoundability	Compoundable [Section 359(1) of BNSS] if offence punishable u/s 303(2). The offence may be compounded by the owner of the stolen property Non-compoundable if punishable under section 112(2)	Non-Compoundable

Sr. No.	Points of comparison	Theft	Snatching
(i)	Summary Trial	Mandatory summary trial if offence is punishable u/s 303(2) and value of stolen property does not exceed ₹ 20,000 [Section 283(1)(i) of BNSS]	Summary trial at Magistrate's discretion when offence is punishable u/s 303(2) [Section 283(2) of BNSS]

Powers of Police and Magistrate to combat snatching

- Provisions of new section 107 of BNSS deal with powers of Police and Magistrate even during the investigation to attach proceeds of crime and powers of Magistrate to distribute the same among victims & forfeit unclaimed proceeds of crime.

SUICIDE, ATTEMPT TO COMMIT SUICIDE [SECTION 309 OF IPC (OMITTED BY BNS)] [1.47]

Suicide

- Hitherto, attempt to commit suicide section 309 of IPC was a punishable offence under section 309 of IPC
- BNS deletes the offence of attempt to commit suicide

SUICIDE, ATTEMPT TO COMMIT SUICIDE TO COMPEL OR RESTRAIN EXERCISE OF LAWFUL POWER [SECTION 226 OF BNS/SECTION 309 OF IPC] [1.48]

Scope of provision

- Section 309 of IPC is now omitted. It is now replaced by section 226 of BNS
- Section 309 of IPC prescribed punishment for any one who attempts to commit suicide and did any act towards the commission of such offence
- Section 226 of BNS prescribes punishment for any one who attempts to commit suicide with the intent to compel or restrain any public servant from discharging his official duty

Community service

- Judge trying the case is given option to award sentence of community service for the offence instead of imprisonment or fine or both

TERRORIST ACT [SECTION 113 OF BNS/SECTIONS 15 TO 21 OF UAPA] [1.49]

BNS v. UAPA

- Section 113 of BNS is a new provision *vis-a-vis* IPC but not *vis-a-vis* UAPA. Section 113 is on the lines of sections 15 to 21 of UAPA,1967

Police officer of rank of SP and above to decide whether offence to be registered under UAPA or under this section.

- For the removal of doubts, it is hereby declared that the officer not below the rank of Superintendent of Police shall decide whether to register the case under this section or under the Unlawful Activities (Prevention) Act, 1967.

Definition of 'terrorist act'

- Section 113(1) defines "terrorist act" as under :
  - Whoever does any act with the intent to threaten or likely to threaten the unity, integrity, sovereignty, security, or economic security of India or with the intent to strike terror or likely to strike terror in the people or any section of the people in India or in any foreign country,—

    (*a*) by using bombs, dynamite or other explosive substance or inflammable substance or firearms or other lethal weapons or poisonous or noxious gases or other chemicals or by any other substance (whether biological, radioactive, nuclear or otherwise) of a hazardous nature or by any other means of whatever nature to cause or likely to cause,—

      (*i*) death of, or injury to, any person or persons; or

      (*ii*) loss of, or damage to, or destruction of, property; or

      (*iii*) disruption of any supplies or services essential to the life of the community in India or in any foreign country; or

      (*iv*) damage to, the monetary stability of India by way of production or smuggling or circulation of counterfeit Indian paper currency, coin or of any other material; or

      (*v*) damage or destruction of any property in India or in a foreign country used or intended to be used for the defence of India or in connection with any other purposes of the Government of India, any State Government or any of their agencies; or

(*b*) overawes by means of criminal force or the show of criminal force or attempts to do so or causes death of any public functionary or attempts to cause death of any public functionary; or

(*c*) detains, kidnaps or abducts any person and threatening to kill or injure such person or does any other act in order to compel the Government of India, any State Government or the Government of a foreign country or an international or inter-governmental organisation or any other person to do or abstain from doing any act,

commit a *terrorist act*.

The definition in section 113(1) is on the same lines as in section 15(1) of UAPA,1967. Section 15(2) of UAPA provides that terrorist act includes an act which constitutes an offence within the scope of, and as defined in any of the treaties specified in the Second Schedule to UAPA. This provision of section 15(2) has not been incorporated in section 113 of BNS.

■ For the purpose of this sub-section,—

(*a*) "public functionary" means the constitutional authorities or any other functionary notified in the Official Gazette by the Central Government as public functionary;

(*b*) "counterfeit Indian currency" means the counterfeit currency as may be declared after examination by an authorised or notified forensic authority that such currency imitates or compromises with the key security features of Indian currency.

Punishment for commission of 'terrorist act'[Section 113(2)]

◆ Whoever commits a terrorist act shall,—

(*a*) if such offence has resulted in the death of any person, be punished with death or imprisonment for life, and shall also be liable to fine;

(*b*) in any other case, be punished with imprisonment for a term which shall not be less than five years but which may extend to imprisonment for life, and shall also be liable to fine. [Section 113(2)]

- Section 113(2) is exactly the same as section 16 of UAPA

Punishment for conspiring/attempting to commit/advocating/ abetting/ advising / inciting or knowingly facilitating the commission of a terrorist act

- Whoever conspires or attempts to commit, or advocates, abets, advises or incites, directly or knowingly facilitates the commission of a terrorist act or any act preparatory to the commission of a terrorist act, shall be punished with imprisonment for a term which shall not be less than five years but which may extend to imprisonment for life, and shall also be liable to fine.[Section 113(3)]
- Section 113(3) is exactly the same as section 18 of UAPA

Punishment for organising camp to train terrorists or recruiting persons for committing terrorist acts

- Whoever organises or causes to be organised any camp or camps for imparting training in terrorist act, *or recruits or causes to be recruited any person or persons for commission of a terrorist act*, shall be punished with imprisonment for a term which shall not be less than five years but which may extend to imprisonment for life, and shall also be liable to fine. [Section 113(4)]
- Section 113(4) merges the provisions of sections 18A and 18B of UAPA into a single provision

Punishment for being a member of organisation involved in terrorist act

- Any person who is a member of an organisation which is involved in terrorist act, shall be punished with imprisonment for a term which may extend to imprisonment for life, and shall also be liable to fine. [Section 113(5)]
- Section 113(5) provides punishment for being a member of organisation involved in terrorist act while section 20 of UAPA relates to punishment for being member of terrorist gang or terrorist organization

Harbouring or concealing a terrorist

- Whoever voluntarily harbours or conceals, or attempts to harbour or conceal any person knowing that such person has committed a terrorist act shall be punished with imprisonment for a term which shall not be less than three years but which may extend to imprisonment for life, and shall also be liable to fine: [Section 113(6)]

- This sub-section shall not apply to any case in which the harbour or concealment is by the spouse of the offender.
- Section 113(6) is on the same lines as section 19 of UAPA. Section 113(6) punishes knowingly harbouring person who has committed a terrorist act while section 19 of UAPA punishes knowingly harbouring a terrorist

Punishment for possessing proceeds of terrorist acts

- Whoever knowingly possesses any property derived or obtained from commission of any terrorist act or acquired through the commission of any terrorist act shall be punished with imprisonment for a term which may extend to imprisonment for life, and shall also be liable to fine.[Section 113(7)]
- Section 21 of UAPA provides that whoever knowingly holds any property derived or obtained from commission of any terrorist act or acquired through the terrorist fund shall be punishable with imprisonment for a term which may extend to imprisonment for life, and shall also be liable to fine.

Powers of Police and Magistrate to combat such crime

- Provisions of new section 107 of BNSS deal with powers of Police and Magistrate even during the investigation to attach proceeds of crime and powers of Magistrate to distribute the same among victims & forfeit unclaimed proceeds of crime. *See* **Forfeiture of property**

THEFT [SECTIONS 303, 112 AND 2(*21*) OF BNS/SECTIONS 378, 379 AND 22 OF IPC] [1.50]

Expanded definition of "theft" vis-a-vis IPC [Section 303(1) read with section 112(1) and section 2(*21*)]

- The definition of "movable property" in BNS is wider than it was in IPC.
- Section 2(*21*) of BNS omits the word "are intended to include corporeal" before the word "property" which was there in the definition of movable property in section 22 of IPC
- Therefore, movable property includes property of every description other than immovable property whether such property is in corporeal (tangible physical) form or not.

- Definition of movable property under BNS will include intangible assets like patents, copyrights, etc., also as well as actionable claims.
- Definition of theft will include data theft also and will cover online stealing of funds by hacking bank accounts.
- In view of expanded definition of movable property, theft will include theft of intangible assets, theft of data, theft through card skimming, online theft through hacking bank accounts or cloning the mobile etc.
- In view of section 3(2) of BNS, the term "theft" in section 303 will also cover offences included in scope of "theft" in the inclusive definition of "theft" in *Explanation* to section 112(1). In terms of the said *Explanation*, "theft" includes trick theft, theft from vehicle, dwelling house or business premises, cargo theft, pick pocketing, theft through card skimming, shoplifting and theft of Automated Teller Machine.

Prescribed punishment [Section 303(2)]

- In normal cases of theft imprisonment remains at 3 years under both old and new law
- In case of repeat offences of thefts (second or subsequent conviction), more stringent punishment is provided for in BNS by way of rigorous imprisonment for a term which shall not be less than one year but which may extend to five years and with fine

Community service as punishment for first-time convict if he returns value of stolen property or restores stolen property

- Proviso to section 303(2) of BNS provides for punishment with community service instead of imprisonment or fine or both in case of petty thefts (value of the stolen property is less than ₹ 5000) by first-time convict upon return of the value of property or restoration of the stolen property

Snatching

- Punishment for theft under section 379 of IPC applied to theft by snatching also. Under BNS, theft by snatching is a separate offence u/s 304 of BNS with more stringent punishment

Mandatory Summary trial of offences of petty theft

- The monetary limits for petty thefts triable in summary trials in terms of value of stolen property involved has been increased from ₹ 2000 (section 260(1) of Cr.PC) to ₹ 20000 [section 283(1) of Bharatiya Nagarik Suraksha Sanhita (BNSS)]

- Section 283 of BNSS makes summary trial mandatory for petty and less serious cases. Under Cr.PC, it was discretionary for the Magistrate to try petty and less serious offences in a summary way as section 260(1) of Cr.PC used the words "may, if he thinks fit, try in a summary way all or any of the following offences". Section 283(1) of BNSS replaces the word "may" with the word "shall" and has also increased monetary limits for petty offences to be tried summarily

When offence of theft is punishable under this section and when punishable u/s 112

- If offence commits theft as a lone wolf (operating by himself solo and not part of gang/group), it will be punishable under this section
- If offender committing "theft" is a member of a gang or group, offence is punishable under section 112 as petty organized crime.

Powers of Police and Magistrate to combat such crime

- Provisions of new section 107 of BNSS deal with powers of Police and Magistrate even during the investigation to attach proceeds of crime and powers of Magistrate to distribute the same among victims & forfeit unclaimed proceeds of crime. See Forfeiture of property

THEFT BY CLERK OR SERVANT OF PROPERTY IN POSSESSION OF MASTER [SECTION 306 OF BNS/SECTION 381 OF IPC] [1.51]

Mandatory Summary trial

- Summary trial of offence under this section is mandatory (see section 283 of BNSS)

THEFT IN A DWELLING HOUSE, OR MEANS OF TRANSPORTATION OR PLACE OF WORSHIP, ETC. [SECTIONS 305 AND 112 OF BNS/SECTION 380 OF IPC] [1.52]

Enlarged definition

- Section 305 of BNS provides a more comprehensive definition of theft by including theft in various settings beyond dwelling houses.
- Section 380 of IPC covers theft in any building, tent or vessel, which building, tent or vessel is used as a human dwelling, or used for the custody of property. However, section 305 of BNS covers theft—

(*a*) in any building, tent or vessel used as a human dwelling or used for the custody of property; or

(*b*) of any means of transport used for the transport of goods or passengers; or

(*c*) of any article or goods from any means of transport used for the transport of goods or passengers; or

(*d*) of idol or icon in any place of worship; or

(*e*) of any property of the Government or of a local authority,

Mandatory Summary trial

- Summary trial of offence under this section is mandatory (see section 283 of BNSS)

When offence of theft from vehicle, dwelling house or business premises is punishable under section 305 and when punishable u/s 112

- If offender committing the offence is a member of a gang or group, the offence is punishable under section 112 as petty organized crime.

TREASON, ACTS ENDANGERING SOVEREIGNTY, UNITY AND INTEGRITY OF INDIA [SECTION 152 OF BNS/SECTION 124A OF IPC] [1.53]

Treason

- BNS has omitted section 124A of IPC under which sedition was a punishable offence.
- Section 124A of IPC provided that whoever by words, either spoken or written, or by signs, or by visible representation, or otherwise, brings or attempts to bring into hatred or contempt, or excites or attempts to excite disaffection towards, the Government established by law in India, shall be punished with imprisonment for life, to which fine may be added, or with imprisonment which may extend to three years, to which fine may be added, or with fine.
- In order to expel the British from the country, thousands of freedom fighters spent the golden years of their lives in jail on charges of sedition. Abolition of this offence in independent India will give satisfaction to their souls [*PIB Press Release, dated 20-12-2023*]
- BNS has replaced sedition with treason. [*PIB Press Release, dated 20-12-2023*].

- A new offence relating to act of endangering sovereignty, unity and integrity of India has been added under section 152 in BNS.
- Unlike IPC, sedition is no longer an offence under BNS.
- Instead, offence under BNS is treason which is covered in section 152 of BNS as acts endangering sovereignty, unity and integrity of India.

Act endangering sovereignty, unity and integrity of India

- ***Section 152 is a new provision.***
- Section 152 of BNS provides that whoever, purposely or knowingly, by words, either spoken or written, or by signs, or by visible representation, or by electronic communication or by use of financial mean, or otherwise, excites or attempts to excite, secession or armed rebellion or subversive activities, or encourages feelings of separatist activities or endangers sovereignty or unity and integrity of India; or indulges in or commits any such act shall be punished with imprisonment for life or with imprisonment which may extend to seven years, and shall also be liable to fine.
- *Explanation* to section 152 of BNS clarifies that comments expressing disapprobation of the measures, or administrative or other action of the Government with a view to obtain their alteration by lawful means without exciting or attempting to excite the activities referred to in this section (activities of secession or armed rebellion or subversive activities, activities of encouraging feelings of separatist activities or endangering sovereignty or unity and integrity of India) do not constitute an offence under this section.

TRICK THEFT [SECTIONS 303 AND 112 OF BNS/SECTIONS 378 AND 379 OF IPC] [1.54]

Trick theft

- Trick theft is specifically included in the definition of "theft" in *Explanation* to section 112(1).
- Any act of theft is petty organised crime if committed, whether singly or jointly, by a member of a group or a gang.

When trick theft is punishable as theft under section 303(2) and when punishable u/s 112(2) as petty organised crime

- If offence commits theft as a lone wolf (operating by himself solo and not part of gang/group), it will be punishable under section 303(2)

- If offender committing "theft" is a member of a gang or group, offence is punishable under section 112 as petty organized crime.

UNNATURAL OFFENCES [SECTION 377 OF IPC (OMITTED BY BNS)] [1.55]

- Section 377 of IPC dealt with unnatural offences.
- This offence has been omitted by BNS.

WEIGHTS AND MEASURES, OFFENCES RELATING TO [SECTIONS 264 TO 267 OF IPC (OMITTED BY BNS)/SECTION 153 OF CRPC (OMITTED BY BNSS] [1.56]

- Chapter XIII of IPC comprising sections 264 to 267 dealt with offences relating to weights and measures. These provisions have become redundant since these matters are covered by Legal Metrology Act, 2009. Therefore, BNS omits these provisions.
- Consequently, BNSS omits section 153 of Cr.PC (Inspection of weights and measures)

WOMAN, ENTICING OR TAKING AWAY OR DETAINING WITH CRIMINAL INTENT A MARRIED WOMAN [SECTION 84 OF BNS/ SECTION 498 OF IPC] [1.57]

Woman under husband care or any other person

- Words 'from that man, or from any person having the care of her on behalf of that man' are omitted from section 498 of IPC
- Thus, unlike section 498 of IPC, offence under section 84 of BNS is committed whether or not a married woman is taken or enticed away from her husband or from any person having care of her on behalf of her husband.
- Section 84 protects a married woman whether or not she is living in the care of her husband or any other person who is taking care of her on behalf of her husband.

DIVISION TWO

UNDERSTANDING CRIMINAL JUSTICE PROCEDURES UNDER BHARATIYA NAGARIK SURAKSHA SANHITA, 2023 (BNSS)

ALPHABETICAL KEY TO UNDERSTANDING CRIMINAL JUSTICE PROCEDURES UNDER BHARATIYA NAGARIK SURAKSHA SANHITA, 2023 (BNSS)

Accused, absence of, provision for inquiries and trial being held in absence of accused in certain cases, ***para 2.1***

- Personal attendance of accused through audio-video electronics means

Adjournments, power to postpone or adjourn proceedings, ***para 2.2***

- Limits on adjournments

Appeals, no appeal in petty cases, ***para 2.3***

- No appeal provision

Arrest, by private person and procedure on such arrest, ***para 2.4***

- Time-limit of handing over arrestee (subjected to private arrest) to police
- Re-arrest by police

Arrest, designated police officer, ***para 2.5***

- Information display

Arrest, examination of accused by medical practitioner at request of police officer, ***para 2.6***

- Request for examination

Arrest, examination of arrested person by medical officer, ***para 2.7***

- Medical examination

Arrest, examination of person accused of rape by medical practitioner, ***para 2.8***

- Request to RMP for medical examination of rape accused

Arrest, how made, ***para 2.9***

- Hand cuffing

Arrest, identity parade (identification of person arrested), ***para 2.10***

- Identification process

Arrest, obligation of person making arrest to inform about arrest, etc., to relative or friend, ***para 2.11***

- Information as to arrest

Arrest, person arrested not to be detained more than twenty-four hours, ***para 2.12***

- Magistrate having jurisdiction or not

Arrest, power to seize offensive weapons, ***para 2.13***

- Seizure of weapons

Arrest, procedure of arrest and duties of officer making arrest, ***para 2.14***

- Information of arrest

Arrest, procedure on arrest of person against whom warrant issued, ***para 2.15***

- Information regarding arrest

Arrest, when may police arrest without a warrant, ***para 2.16***

- Arrest of Infirm/Old age person where offence is punishable with imprisonment of less than 3 years

Assistant public prosecutors, ***para 2.17***

- Notice to State Government

Attachment, forfeiture or restoration of property, ***para 2.18***

- Attachment, forfeiture, etc.

Audio video electronic means, ***para 2.19***

- General
- Use of any communication device
- "Communication device" means mobile phones
- Such other means as the State Government may, by rules provide

Bail, anticipatory bail (direction for grant of bail to person apprehending arrest), ***para 2.20***

- Anticipatory bail

Bail, when bail can be taken in case of non-bailable offence, ***para 2.21***

- In case of a child/woman/sick or infirm
- Refusal for bail

Bails, maximum period for which undertrial prisoner can be detained, ***para 2.22***

- Undertrial prisoner

Charges, framing of charge, ***para 2.23***

- Time-bound framing of charges in warrant cases trials

Charges - Joinder of - Offences of same kind within year may be charged together, ***para 2.24***

- Number of offences

Cognizable offences, preliminary inquiry in, ***para 2.25***

- Preliminary enquiry

Complainant, absence of, ***para 2.26***

- Discharge of accused if complainant absent and offence is compoundable or is not a cognizable offence

Contempt cases, procedure in certain cases of contempt, ***para 2.27***

- Fine prescribed

Court of session, commitment of case to Court of session when offence is triable exclusively by it, ***para 2.28***

- Time limit for completion of proceedings
- Copy to Court of Sessions

Court of session, supply of copies of statements and documents to accused in other cases triable by Court of session, ***para 2.29***

- Time limit and form for supply of copy

Court of session, trial before, discharge, ***para 2.30***

- Time-limit for making application for discharge

Court of session, trial before, framing of charge, ***para 2.31***

- Time-frame for framing of charges
- Accused presence in Court electronically

Court of session, trial before, evidence for prosecution, ***para 2.32***

- Recording of witness, etc., by audio-video electronic means

Evidence, mode of taking, evidence to be taken in presence of accused, ***para 2.43***

- Audio-video electronic means

Evidence, mode of taking, record of examination of accused, ***para 2.44***

- Time limit for taking signature of accused examined by electronic communication

Forensic evidence collection for serious offences, mandatory, ***para 2.45***

- Forensic evidence collection centre

Handwriting, signature specimen, power of magistrate to order person to give specimen signatures or handwriting, etc., ***para 2.46***

- Magistrate's power to order any person to give specimen signature, etc.

In camera trial, ***para 2.47***

- In camera trial provision extended to offences under Protection of Children from Sexual Offences Act also

Investigation, ***para 2.48***

- Investigation

Judgment, ***para 2.49***

- Time limit for pronouncing judgment by Court
- Time-limit for loading copy of Court's judgment on its portal
- Accused in custody to hear judgment by audio-video electronic means

Magistrate, cognizance of offences by, ***para 2.50***

- Mode of taking cognizance

Magistrate, examination of complainant, ***para 2.51***

- Cognizance of complaint

Mercy petition in death sentence cases, ***para 2.52***

- Mercy petition

Metropolitan area/metropolitan magistrate, ***para 2.53***

- Metropolitan Magistrate

Offence committed outside India, ***para 2.54***

- Offence committed outside India

Online FIR, ***para 2.55***

- Online FIR for cognizable offences : Information of cognizable offence can be given to police by electronic communication

Plea bargaining, application for plea bargaining, ***para 2.56***

- Time-limit for filing application for plea bargaining
- Time-limit for reaching a mutually satisfactory disposition

Plea bargaining, disposal of case, ***para 2.57***

- First time offender

Police, cases to be sent to magistrate, when evidence is sufficient, ***para 2.58***

- Security for appearance

Police, information to, information as to non-cognizable cases and investigation of such cases, ***para 2.59***

- Daily diary

Police, information to, information in cognizable cases, ***para 2.60***

- Introduction of "Zero FIRs" for cognizable offences
- Online FIR for cognizable offences : Information of cognizable offence can be given to police by electronic communication
- Information to informant/victim
- Preliminary enquiry
- Powers of Superintendent of Police

Police, medical examination of victim of rape, ***para 2.61***

- Time-limit for submission of medical examination report of rape victim

Police, persons bound to conform to lawful directions of police, ***para 2.62***

- Binding force of lawful directions of Police

Police, police officer's power to require attendance of witnesses, ***para 2.63***

- Acute illness
- Exempted person willingness to attend

Police, police to enquire and report on suicide, etc., ***para 2.64***

- Time-limit for sending enquiry report to DM/SDM

Police, power to investigate, police officer's power to investigate cognizable case, ***para 2.65***

- Powers of Superintendent of Police/Judicial Magistrate

Police, power to investigate, procedure for investigation, ***para 2.66***

- Mandatory recording of rape victim's statement through Audio-video electronic means
- Mandatory Forensic Evidence Collection for Serious Offences
- Non-compliance with requirement of section 176(1)

Police, power to summon persons, ***para 2.67***

- Restrictions on power to summon persons

Police, procedure when investigation cannot be completed in 24 hours, ***para 2.68***

- Period of declaration
- Detention in police station
- Audio-video electronic means

Police, recording of confessions and statements, ***para 2.69***

- Woman Magistrate
- Recording statement of witness
- Audio-video electronic means

Police, report of police officer on completion of investigation, ***para 2.70***

- Requirement of time-bound completion of investigation within 2 months applicable to offences of rape and gang rape have been extended to offences under POCSO
- Electronic communication
- Progress of investigation
- Mandatory Submission of copies of documents to Magistrate by investigating officer for supply of the same to accused
- Time-limit for completion of investigation

Police report, supply to accused of copy of police report and other documents, ***para 2.71***

- Time limit stipulated for supply of copy of police report, FIR etc.
- Copy to victim
- Report in electronic form

Proclaimed offender, identification and attachment of property of proclaimed person, ***para 2.72***

- Attachment of property

Proclaimed offender, inquiry, trial or judgment in absentia of proclaimed offender, ***para 2.73***

- Deemed joint trial [Section 24 of BSA]

Proclaimed offender - Police, duty of officers employed in connection with affairs of a village to make a certain report, ***para 2.74***

- Proclaimed offender

Property, disposal of, order for custody and disposal of property pending trial in certain cases, ***para 2.75***

- Magistrate
- Statement of property
- Photograph/videography of property
- Time limit for disposal of property

Property, power to sell perishable property, ***para 2.76***

- Prescribed value

Prosecution, withdrawal from, ***para 2.77/78***

- Opportunity of hearing to victim before allowing withdrawal of prosecution

Public nuisance, Magistrate may prohibit the repetition or continuance of public nuisance, ***para 2.79***

- Deputy Commissioner of Police

Public nuisance, person to whom order is addressed to obey or show cause, ***para 2.80***

- Audio video conference

Public nuisance, procedure where person against whom order is made appears to show cause, ***para 2.81***

- Time-limit for completion of proceedings

Public order and tranquility, dispersal of assembly by use of civil force, ***para 2.82***

- Provision made gender neutral

Public order and tranquility, use of armed forces to disperse assembly, ***para 2.83***

- District/Executive Magistrate

Public prosecutors, ***para 2.84***

- Public prosecutors for National Territory of Delhi Region
- Special Public Prosecutor

Public servants, evidence of public servants, experts, public officers in certain cases, ***para 2.85***

- Successor officer/expert

Public servant, prosecution for contempt of lawful authority of public servants, for offences against public justice and for offences relating to documents given in evidence, ***para 2.86***

- Cognizance by whom

Public servant, prosecution of judges and public servants, ***para 2.87***

- Time limit for sanction

Search, mobile recording, ***para 2.88***

- Mandatory recording of search by mobile phone
- Time limit for sending records

Search, mobile recording, audio video electronic means, recording of search and seizure through audio-video electronic means, ***para 2.89***

- Recording of search & seizure by mobile phone

Security for good behaviour from habitual offenders, ***para 2.90***

- Specified Acts

Sentence commutation of, power to commute sentence, ***para 2.91***

- Commutation of sentences

Sentences, in cases of conviction of several offences at one trial, ***para 2.92***

- Court to clearly spell out in order whether punishments to run consecutively or concurrently after considering the gravity of the offences
- Maximum punishment for imprisonment for life

Sentences, which High Courts and sessions judges may pass, ***para 2.93***

- Assistant Sessions Judge

Sentences, which magistrates may pass, ***para 2.94***

- Monetary limits on fines
- Metropolitan Area/Metropolitan Magistrate

- Community service
- Offences for which punishment of community service can be awarded

Special Executive Magistrates, ***para 2.95***

- Police officer

Summary trials, power to try summarily, ***para 2.96***

- Mandatory summary trial for petty and less serious cases

Summons, form of, ***para 2.97***

- Electronic summons

Summons, how served, ***para 2.98***

- Summons by electronic communication
- Record keeping

Summons, issue of process, ***para 2.99***

- Electronic summons

Summons, non-appearance or death of complainant, ***para 2.100***

- Acquittal of accused for non-appearance of complainant

Summons, proof of service in such cases and when serving officer not present, ***para 2.101***

- Summons by electronic communication

Summons, service of summons on corporate bodies, firms and societies, ***para 2.102***

- Service of summons to firm, or association of individuals other than company or corporation

Summons, service of summons on witness, ***para 2.103***

- Summons by electronic communication

Summons, substance of accusation to be stated, ***para 2.104***

- Release of accused

Trial and proceedings to be held in electronic mode, ***para 2.105***

Victims, treatment of, ***para 2.106***

- Duty of hospitals to provide immediately, the first-aid or medical treatment, free of cost to victims of offences under Protection of Children from Sexual Offences Act, 2012

UNDERSTANDING CRIMINAL JUSTICE PROCEDURES UNDER BHARATIYA NAGARIK SURAKSHA SANHITA, 2023 (BNSS)

ACCUSED, ABSENCE OF, PROVISION FOR INQUIRIES AND TRIAL BEING HELD IN ABSENCE OF ACCUSED IN CERTAIN CASES [SECTION 355 OF BNSS/SECTION 317 OF Cr.PC.] [2.1]

Personal attendance of accused through audio-video electronics means

- Newly added *Explanation* to section 355 provides that personal attendance of the accused includes attendance through audio-video electronic means.

ADJOURNMENTS, POWER TO POSTPONE OR ADJOURN PROCEEDINGS [SECTION 346 OF BNSS/SECTION 309 OF Cr.PC.] [2.2]

Limits on adjournments

- Section 346(2), fourth proviso, of BNSS provides that where the circumstances are beyond the control of a party, not more than two adjournments may be granted by the court after hearing the objections of the other party and for the reasons to be recorded in writing
- Under section 309 of Cr.PC, there was no limit on power of Court to grant adjournments if circumstances are beyond the control of a party seeking adjournment

APPEALS, NO APPEAL IN PETTY CASES [SECTION 417 OF BNSS/ SECTION 376 OF Cr.PC.] [2.3]

No appeal provision

- Section 376(*a*) of Cr.PC provided that there shall no appeal by a convicted person where a High Court passes only a sentence of imprisonment for a term not exceeding *six months* or of fine not exceeding one thousand rupees, or of both such imprisonment and fine
- Section 417(1)(*a*) of BNSS has modified above provisions so as to provide that there shall no appeal by a convicted person where a High Court passes only a sentence of imprisonment for a term not exceeding *three months* or of fine not exceeding *one thousand rupees*, or of both such imprisonment and fine

ARREST, BY PRIVATE PERSON AND PROCEDURE ON SUCH ARREST [SECTION 40 OF BNSS/SECTION 43 OF Cr.PC.] [2.4]

Time-limit of handing over arrestee (subjected to private arrest) to police

- Section 43(1) of Cr.PC did not set any time-limit for handing over to the Police of the person subjected to private arrest. It only provided that handing over arrestee to the Police should be without *unnecessary delay*.
- Section 40 of BNSS makes changes to private arrest provisions by setting a deadline of *6 hours* from such arrest within which the private person effecting private arrest shall hand over the person subjected to private arrest to the Police.
- Section 40 however does not say what the private person is to do if he is unable to hand over the person subjected to private arrest to the Police within the 6 hours deadline due to some unavoidable reasons.

Re-arrest by police

- Section 43(2) of Cr.PC provided that if there is reason to believe that such person comes under the provisions relating to Police arrest, a police officer shall re-arrest him. The Police taking custody of person subjected to private arrest was termed as "*re-arrest*" under Cr.PC provisions.

- Section 40(2) of BNSS has substituted the words "shall re-arrest him" with the words '*shall take him to custody*'. In other words, section 40 provides that Police taking custody of privately arrested person is not "re-arrest" but only 'taking him in custody'.

ARREST, DESIGNATED POLICE OFFICER [SECTION 37 OF BNSS/ SECTION 41C OF Cr.PC] [2.5]

Information display

- Section 41C of the Cr.PC provided that the State Government shall cause to be displayed on the notice board kept outside the control rooms at every district, the names and addresses of the persons arrested and the name and designation of the police officers who made the arrests.

  The control room at the Police Headquarters at the State level shall collect from time to time, details about the persons arrested, nature of the offence with which they are charged and maintain a database for the information of the general public.

- Section 37 of the BNSS provides that the State Government shall designate a police officer in every district and in every police station, not below the rank of Assistant Sub-Inspector of Police who shall be responsible for maintaining the information about the names and addresses of the persons arrested, nature of the offence with which charged, which shall be prominently displayed in any manner including in digital mode in every police station and at the district headquarters.

ARREST, EXAMINATION OF ACCUSED BY MEDICAL PRACTITIONER AT REQUEST OF POLICE OFFICER [SECTION 51 OF BNSS/SECTION 53 OF Cr.PC.] [2.6]

Request for examination

- Under section 53 of the Cr.PC request for medical examination can be made by police officer not below the rank of sub-inspector.
- Under section 51(1) of the BNSS request can be made by *any* police officer.

ARREST, EXAMINATION OF ARRESTED PERSON BY MEDICAL OFFICER [SECTION 53 OF BNSS/SECTION 54 OF Cr.PC.] [2.7]

Medical examination

- Section 54 of Cr.PC provided that when any person is arrested, he shall be examined by a medical officer in the service of Central or State Government, and in case the medical officer is not available, by a registered medical practitioner soon after the arrest is made.
- Section 53 of BNSS has made changes to these provisions by inserting a proviso in section 53(1). The said proviso provides that if the medical officer or the registered medical practitioner is of the opinion that one more examination of arrested female is necessary, he may do so.

ARREST, EXAMINATION OF PERSON ACCUSED OF RAPE BY MEDICAL PRACTITIONER [SECTION 52 OF BNSS/SECTION 53A OF Cr.PC.] [2.8]

Request to RMP for medical examination of rape accused

- Section 53A(1) of Cr.PC provided that where there is no Registered Medical Practitioner (RMP) employed in a hospital run by the Government or by a local authority within the radius of sixteen kilometres from the place where the offence of rape has been committed, it shall be lawful for any other RMP to make an examination of the rape accused on receiving request of a police officer *not below the rank of a sub-inspector*.
- Section 52 of BNSS modifies above provisions and allows such RMP to act on the request of *any* Police Officer *irrespective of rank*.

ARREST, HOW MADE [SECTION 43 OF BNSS/SECTION 46 OF Cr.PC.] [2.9]

Hand cuffing

- The provisions of section 46 of Cr.PC did not provide for manner of making arrest. It does not provide any guidelines on when arrestee may be handcuffed. Section 43(3) of BNSS fills this gap.

- Section 43(3) of BNSS provides that the police officer may, keeping in view the nature and gravity of the offence, use handcuff while effecting the arrest of a person who is a habitual, repeat offender who escaped from custody, who has committed offence of organised crime, offence of terrorist act, drug related crime, or offence of illegal possession of arms and ammunition, murder, rape, acid attack, counterfeiting of coins and currency notes, human trafficking, sexual offences against children, or offences against the State.

ARREST, IDENTITY PARADE (IDENTIFICATION OF PERSON ARRESTED) [SECTION 54 OF BNSS/SECTION 54A OF Cr.PC.] [2.10]

Identification process

- Section 54A of Cr.PC provides that if the person identifying the person arrested is mentally or physically disabled, the identification process shall be *videographed*.
- Section 54 of BNSS modifies above provision to require recording of identification process by *any audio-video electronic means* (e.g. *mobile)* instead of earlier requirement of videographing the identity parade.

ARREST, OBLIGATION OF PERSON MAKING ARREST TO INFORM ABOUT ARREST, ETC., TO RELATIVE OR FRIEND [SECTION 48 OF BNSS/SECTION 50A OF Cr.PC.] [2.11]

Information as to arrest

- Section 48 of BNSS stipulates a new requirement that information of arrest and place where the arrestee is held shall be given to the designated police officer in the district.

ARREST, PERSON ARRESTED NOT TO BE DETAINED MORE THAN TWENTY-FOUR HOURS [SECTION 58 OF BNSS/SECTION 57 OF Cr.PC.] [2.12]

Magistrate having jurisdiction or not

- Section 57 of Cr.PC provided that no police officer shall detain in custody a person arrested without warrant for a longer period than under all the circumstances of the case is reasonable, and such period shall not, in the absence of a special order of a Magistrate, exceed 24 hours exclusive of the time necessary for the journey from the place of arrest to the Magistrate's Court.

- Section 58 of BNSS modifies the above provisions to provide that Police detention shall not exceed 24 hours exclusive of the time necessary for the journey from the place of arrest to the Magistrate's Court, *whether having jurisdiction* or not.
- The words in italics added at the end of the provision in section 58 seems to require the Police to produce every arrestee as soon as possible before the nearest Magistrate, whether jurisdictional Magistrate or not.

ARREST, POWER TO SEIZE OFFENSIVE WEAPONS [SECTION 50 OF BNSS/ SECTION 52 OF Cr.PC.] [2.13]

Seizure of weapons

- Section 50 of BNSS empowers the Police Officer or other person making the arrest to seize offensive weapons from the arrestee *immediately after the arrest is made*. Section 52 of Cr.PC offered no clarity on when this power is exercisable.

ARREST, PROCEDURE OF ARREST AND DUTIES OF OFFICER MAKING ARREST [SECTION 36 OF BNSS/SECTION 41B OF Cr.PC.] [2.14]

Information of arrest

- Section 41B of the Cr.PC required the information of arrest to be given to 'relative or friend' named by person arrested
- Section 36 of the BNSS requires the information of arrest be given to 'relative or a friend or *any other person*' named by person arrested

ARREST, PROCEDURE ON ARREST OF PERSON AGAINST WHOM WARRANT ISSUED [SECTION 82 OF BNSS/SECTION 80 OF Cr.PC.] [2.15]

Information regarding arrest

- Section 82(2) of BNSS additionally provides for a new requirement that on the arrest of any person against whom warrant is issued, the police officer shall forthwith give the information regarding such arrest and the place where the arrested person is being held to the designated police officer in the district and to such officer of another district where the arrested person normally resides.

ARREST, WHEN MAY POLICE ARREST WITHOUT A WARRANT [SECTION 35 OF BNSS/SECTIONS 41 AND 41A OF Cr.PC.] [2.16]

Arrest of Infirm/Old age person where offence is punishable with imprisonment of less than 3 years

- ***Section 35(7) of BNSS is a new provision*** **[NEW]**
- New sub-section (7) of section 35 provides that no arrest shall be made without the prior permission of an officer not below the rank of Deputy Superintendent of Police in cases where the offence is punishable with imprisonment for less than three years, and the person is infirm or above sixty years of age.

ASSISTANT PUBLIC PROSECUTORS [SECTION 19 OF BNSS/ SECTION 25 OF Cr.PC.] [2.17]

Notice to State Government

- Section 19 of the BNSS stipulates a new requirement that provides that when no Assistant Public Prosecutor is available District Magistrate may exercise his power of appointment of any other person as Assistant Public Prosecutor after giving notice of 14 days to the State Government

ATTACHMENT, FORFEITURE OR RESTORATION OF PROPERTY [SECTION 107 OF BNSS] [2.18]

Attachment, forfeiture, etc.

- ***Section 107 of the BNSS is a new provision*** **[NEW]**
- Section 107 provides as under:

  1. Where a police officer making an investigation has reason to believe that any property is derived or obtained, directly or indirectly, as a result of a criminal activity or from the commission of any offence, he may, with the approval of the Superintendent of Police or Commissioner of Police, make an application to the Court or the Judicial Magistrate exercising jurisdiction to take cognizance of the offence or commit for trial or try the case, for the attachment of such property.

2. If the Court or the Judicial Magistrate has reasons to believe, whether before or after taking evidence, that all or any of such properties are proceeds of crime, the Court or the Magistrate may issue a notice upon such person calling upon him to show cause within a period of fourteen days as to why an order of attachment shall not be made.
3. Where the notice issued to any person in (*2*) above specifies any property as being held by any other person on behalf of such person, a copy of the notice shall also be served upon such other person.
4. The Court or the Judicial Magistrate may, after considering the explanation, if any, to the show-cause notice issued as above and the material fact available before such Court or Magistrate and after giving a reasonable opportunity of being heard to such person or persons, may pass an order of attachment, in respect of those properties which are found to be the proceeds of crime.

   If such person does not appear before the Court or the Magistrate or represent his case before the Court or Judicial Magistrate within a period of fourteen days specified in the show-cause notice, the Court or the Judicial Magistrate may proceed to pass the *ex parte* order.
5. If the Court or the Judicial Magistrate is of the opinion that issuance of notice under the said sub-section would defeat the object of attachment or seizure, the Court or Judicial Magistrate may by an interim order passed *ex parte* direct attachment or seizure of such property, and such order shall remain in force till an order in (*6*) below is passed.
6. If the Court or the Judicial Magistrate finds the attached or seized properties to be the proceeds of crime, the Court or the Judicial Magistrate shall by order direct the District Magistrate to rateably distribute such proceeds of crime to the persons who are affected by such crime.
7. On receipt of an order passed in (*6*) above, the District Magistrate shall, within a period of sixty days distribute the proceeds of crime either by himself or authorise any officer subordinate to him to effect such distribution.

8. If there are no claimants to receive such proceeds or no claimant is ascertainable or there is any surplus after satisfying the claimants, such proceeds of crime shall stand forfeited to the Government.

For the purposes of this section, the word "property" and the expression "proceeds of crime" shall have the meaning assigned to them in clause (*d*) and clause (*c*) of section 111 of BNSS.

AUDIO VIDEO ELECTRONIC MEANS [SECTION 2(1)(*a*) OF BNSS] [NEW DEFINITION] [2.19]

General

- Section 2(1)(*a*) of the BNSS defines "audio-video electronic means". It is a new definition introduced by BNSS.

Use of any communication device

- In BNSS, unless the context otherwise requires, the term "audio-video electronic means" shall include use of any communication device for the purposes of—
  - Video conferencing
  - Recording of processes of identification
  - Search and seizure or evidence
  - Transmission of electronic communication, and
  - For such other purposes and by such other means as the State Government may, by rules provide

"Communication device" means mobile phones

- The word "communication device" is not defined in section 2(*1*).
- In view of section 2(*2*) of BNSS, the definition given in the Information Technology Act, 2000 will apply for BNSS purposes.
- "Communication device" means cell phones, personal digital assistance or combination of both or any other device used to communicate, send or transmit any text, video, audio or image [Section 2(*1*)(*ha*) of Information Technology Act,2000]
- BNSS seeks to make evidence recorded on mobile phones admissible as evidence.
- BNSS seeks to permit the use of mobile phones for the purposes of video conferencing, recording of processes of identification, search and seizure or evidence, transmission of electronic

communication and for such other purposes as the State Government may, by rules provide

Such other means as the State Government may, by rules provide

- Apart from mobile phones, the scope of "Audio-video electronic means" covers such other means as the State Government may, by rules provide for above-mentioned purposes. [*See* Section 530 of BNSS]
- This allows State Government to take advantage of advancements in technology without having to amend the Act which is a time-consuming process.
- The State can simply notify use of such advancement to fast-track criminal procedure and make the criminal justice system more hassle-free

BAIL, ANTICIPATORY BAIL (DIRECTION FOR GRANT OF BAIL TO PERSON APPREHENDING ARREST) [SECTION 482 OF BNSS/ SECTION 438 OF Cr.PC.] [2.20]

Anticipatory bail

- Section 438(1) of Cr.PC provided that where any person has reason to believe that he may be arrested on accusation of having committed a non-bailable offence, he may apply to the High Court or the Court of Session for a direction under this section that in the event of such arrest he shall be released on bail; and that Court may, after taking into consideration, *inter alia*, the following factors, namely:—

  (*i*) the nature and gravity of the accusation;

  (*ii*) the antecedents of the applicant including the fact as to whether he has previously undergone imprisonment on conviction by a Court in respect of any cognizable offence;

  (*iii*) the possibility of the applicant to flee from justice; and

  (*iv*) where the accusation has been made with the object of injuring or humiliating the applicant by having him so arrested,

  either reject the application forthwith or issue an interim order for the grant of anticipatory bail.

- Corresponding provisions in BNSS are contained in section 482 of BNSS. Section 482(1) omits factors in (*i*) to (*iv*) above to be considered by the Court for grant of anticipatory bail.

- Section 482(1) of BNSS provides that Court may, *if it thinks fit*, direct that in the event of such arrest, he shall be released on bail.
- Proviso to section 438(1) of Cr.PC. providing that where the High Court or, as the case may be, the Court of Session, has not passed any interim order under this sub-section or has rejected the application for grant of anticipatory bail, it shall be open to an officer-in-charge of a police station to arrest, without warrant the applicant on the basis of the accusation apprehended in such application, *is now omitted.*
- Sub-section (1A) of section 438 of Cr.PC. providing that where the Court grants an interim order under sub-section (1), it shall forthwith cause a notice being not less than seven days notice, together with a copy of such order to be served on the Public Prosecutor and the Superintendent of Police, with a view to give the Public Prosecutor a reasonable opportunity of being heard when the application shall be finally heard by the Court, *is now omitted.*
- Sub-section (1B) of section 438 of Cr.PC. providing that the presence of the applicant seeking anticipatory bail shall be obligatory at the time of final hearing of the application and passing of final order by the Court, if on an application made to it by the Public Prosecutor, the Court considers such presence necessary in the interest of justice, *is now omitted.*

BAIL, WHEN BAIL CAN BE TAKEN IN CASE OF NON-BAILABLE OFFENCE [SECTION 480 OF BNSS/SECTION 437 OF Cr.PC.]

[2.21]

In case of a child/woman/sick or infirm

- Section 437 of Cr.PC provided for denial of bail to a person accused or suspected of commission of non-bailable offence in the following two cases:
  - (*i*) if there appear reasonable grounds for believing that he has been guilty of an offence punishable with death or imprisonment for life;
  - (*ii*) if such offence is a cognizable offence and he had been previously convicted of an offence punishable with death, imprisonment for life or imprisonment for seven years or more, or he had been previously convicted on two or more occasions of a cognizable offence punishable with

imprisonment for three years or more but not less than seven years.

To the above rule of bail denial, there was an exception. First proviso to section 437(1) provided that Court may direct such person to be released on bail if such person is under the age of *sixteen years* or is a woman or is sick or infirm. Section 480 of BNSS modifies the above exception to bail denial by providing that Court may direct that such person be released on bail if such person is a *child* or is a woman or is sick or infirm.

Refusal for bail

- Section 437(1), 2nd proviso, of Cr.PC provided that the mere fact that an accused person may be required for being identified by witnesses during investigation shall not be sufficient ground for refusing to grant bail if he is otherwise entitled to be released on bail and gives an undertaking that he shall comply with such directions as may be given by the Court.
- Section 480, 3rd proviso, of BNSS now provides that the mere fact that an accused person may be required for being identified by witnesses during investigation *or for police custody beyond the first fifteen days* shall not be sufficient ground for refusing to grant bail if he is otherwise entitled to be released on bail and gives an undertaking that he shall comply with such directions as may be given by the Court.

BAILS, MAXIMUM PERIOD FOR WHICH UNDERTRIAL PRISONER CAN BE DETAINED [SECTION 479 OF BNSS/SECTION 436A OF Cr.PC.] [2.22]

Undertrial prisoner

- Section 436A of Cr.PC provided for the maximum period for which an undertrial prisoner can be detained
- Section 479 of BNSS corresponds to section 436A of Cr.PC and makes the following changes in provisions:
  - Section 436A of Cr.PC was not applicable to an offence for which punishment of death has been specified as one of the punishment. Section 479 of BNSS is not applicable to an offence for which punishment of death or *life imprisonment* has been specified as punishment.
  - Where such person is a first-time offender (who has never been convicted of any offence in the past) he shall be released

on bail by the Court, if he has undergone detention for the period extending up to one-third of the maximum period of imprisonment specified for such offence under that law. [First proviso to section 479(1)]

- Where an investigation, inquiry or trial in more than one offence or in multiple cases are pending against a person, he shall not be released on bail by the Court. [Section 479(2)]
- The Superintendent of jail, where the accused person is detained, on completion of one-half or one-third of the maximum period of imprisonment specified for offence under that law, as the case may be, shall forthwith make an application in writing to the Court to proceed under section 479(1) for the release of such person on bail. [Section 479(3)]

CHARGES, FRAMING OF CHARGE [SECTION 263 OF BNSS/ SECTION 240 OF Cr.PC.] [2.23]

Time-bound framing of charges in warrant cases trials

- If, upon such consideration, examination, if any, and hearing, the Magistrate is of opinion that there is ground for presuming that the accused has committed an offence triable under this Chapter, which such Magistrate is competent to try and which, in his opinion, could be adequately punished by him, he shall frame in writing a charge against the accused within a *period of sixty days* from the date of first hearing on charge. No such time-limit was there in section 240 of Cr.PC

CHARGES - JOINDER OF - OFFENCES OF SAME KIND WITHIN YEAR MAY BE CHARGED TOGETHER [SECTION 242 OF BNSS/ SECTION 219 OF Cr.PC.] [2.24]

Number of offences

- Number of offences of same kind within a year that may be charged together has been *increased* from *three to five*

COGNIZABLE OFFENCES, PRELIMINARY INQUIRY IN [SECTION 173 OF BNSS/SECTION 154 OF Cr.PC.] [2.25]

Preliminary enquiry [NEW]

- Section 173(3) is a new provision.

- It provides that without prejudice to the provisions contained in section 175, on receipt of information relating to the commission of any cognizable offence, which is made punishable for three years or more but less than seven years, the officer in-charge of the police station may with the prior permission from an officer not below the rank of Deputy Superintendent of Police, considering the nature and gravity of the offence,—
  - (*i*) proceed to conduct preliminary enquiry to ascertain whether there exists a *prima facie* case for proceeding in the matter within a period of fourteen days; or
  - (*ii*) proceed with investigation when there exists a *prima facie* case.
- There was no provision along these lines in section 154 of Cr.PC

COMPLAINANT, ABSENCE OF [SECTION 272 OF BNSS/SECTION 249 OF Cr.PC.] [2.26]

Discharge of accused if complainant absent and offence is compoundable or is not a cognizable offence

- When the proceedings have been instituted upon complaint, and on any day fixed for the hearing of the case, the complainant is absent, and the offence may be lawfully compounded or is not a cognizable offence, the Magistrate may after giving *thirty days'* time to the complainant to be present, in his discretion, notwithstanding anything hereinbefore contained, at any time before the charge has been framed, discharge the accused. There was no such time-limit under section 249 of the Cr.PC

CONTEMPT CASES, PROCEDURE IN CERTAIN CASES OF CONTEMPT [SECTION 384 OF BNSS/SECTION 345 OF Cr.PC.] [2.27]

Fine prescribed

- Section 345 of Cr.PC. provided that when any offence of contempt of lawful authority of public servants committed in view of any Civil, Criminal or Revenue Court, the Court may cause the offender to be detained in custody, and may, at any time before the rising of the Court or the same day, take cognizance of the offence and, after giving the offender a reasonable opportunity of showing cause why he should not be punished, sentence the offender to fine not exceeding ₹ 200, and, in default of payment of fine, to simple imprisonment for a term which may extend to one month, unless such fine be sooner paid

- Section 384 of BNSS has increased maximum fine imposable for such offence from ₹ 200 to ₹ 1000

COURT OF SESSION, COMMITMENT OF CASE TO COURT OF SESSION WHEN OFFENCE IS TRIABLE EXCLUSIVELY BY IT [SECTION 232 OF BNSS/SECTION 209 OF Cr.PC.] [2.28]

Time limit for completion of proceedings

- Proceedings have been made time-bound. The proceedings under this section shall be completed within a period of ninety days from the date of taking cognizance, and such period may be extended by the Magistrate for a period not exceeding 180 days for the reasons to be recorded in writing [First proviso to Section 232]

Copy to Court of Sessions

- Any application filed before the Magistrate by the accused or the victim or any person authorised by such person in a case triable by Court of Session, shall be forwarded to the Court of Session with the committal of the case. [Second proviso to Section 232]

COURT OF SESSION, SUPPLY OF COPIES OF STATEMENTS AND DOCUMENTS TO ACCUSED IN OTHER CASES TRIABLE BY COURT OF SESSION [SECTION 231 OF BNSS/SECTION 208 OF Cr.PC.] [2.29]

Time limit and form for supply of copy

- The words "without delay" have been replaced by the word "forthwith".
- Second proviso to section 231 provides that supply of documents in electronic form shall be considered as duly furnished.

COURT OF SESSION, TRIAL BEFORE, DISCHARGE [SECTION 250 OF BNSS/SECTION 227 OF Cr.PC.] [2.30]

Time-limit for making application for discharge

- Under section 250(1) of BNSS accused may prefer an application for discharge within a period of 60 days from the date of committal under section 232. There was no such provision in section 227 of the Cr.PC

COURT OF SESSION, TRIAL BEFORE, FRAMING OF CHARGE [SECTION 251 OF BNSS/SECTION 228 OF Cr.PC.] [2.31]

Time-frame for framing of charges

- Section 251(1)(*b*) of BNSS provides that if the Judge is of opinion that there is ground for presuming that the accused has committed an offence which is exclusively triable by Court, he shall frame in writing a charge against the accused within a period of *60 days* from the date of first hearing on charge

Accused presence in Court electronically

- Chargesheet shall be read and explained to accused. For this purpose, accused's physical presence is no more required by section 251. Section 251(2) allows charges to be read and explained even when accused is present in Court through audio-video electronic means

COURT OF SESSION, TRIAL BEFORE, EVIDENCE FOR PROSECUTION [SECTION 254 OF BNSS/SECTION 231 OF Cr.PC.] [2.32]

Recording of witness, etc., by audio-video electronic means

- Proviso to section 254 of BNSS provides that evidence of a witness may be recorded by audio-video electronic means
- The deposition of evidence of any police officer or public servant may be taken through audio-video electronic means

COURT OF SESSION, TRIAL BEFORE, JUDGMENT OF ACQUITTAL OR CONVICTION [SECTION 258 OF BNSS/SECTION 235 OF Cr.PC.] [2.33]

Time-frames for pronouncing judgments

- BNSS prescribes time-frame for judges to pronounce judgments, ensuring timely resolution of cases.

Time-bound disposal of case by conviction or acquittal

- After hearing arguments and points of law (if any), the Judge shall give a judgment in the case, as soon as possible, within a period of *thirty days* from the date of completion of arguments, which may for specific reasons extend to a period of 45 days for reasons to be recorded in writing.

COURT OF SESSION, TRIAL BEFORE, PROCEDURE IN CASES INSTITUTED UNDER SUB-SECTION (2) OF SECTION 222 [SECTION 260 OF BNSS/SECTION 237 OF Cr.PC.] [2.34]

Quantum of compensation where accused acquitted and Court is satisfied that there was no reasonable basis for the accusation

- Quantum of compensation under section 237(4) of Cr.PC. increased from ₹ 1000 to ₹ 5000 in section 260(4) of BNSS.

DEATH SENTENCE, PROCEDURE IN CASES SUBMITTED TO HIGH COURT FOR CONFIRMATION [SECTION 412 OF BNSS/ SECTION 371 OF CR.PC.] [2.35]

Electronic means

- Section 371 of Cr.PC provided that in cases submitted by the Court of Session to the High Court for the confirmation of a sentence of death, the proper officer of the High Court shall, without delay, after the order of confirmation or other order has been made by the High Court, send a copy of the order, under the seal of the High Court and attested with his official signature, to the Court of Session
- Section 412 of the BNSS has modified above provisions to provide that the order of High Court may be sent to Court of session by the proper Officer of High Court *either physically or through electronic means.*

DEATH SENTENCE, SENTENCE OF DEATH TO BE SUBMITTED BY COURT OF SESSION FOR CONFIRMATION [SECTION 407 OF BNSS/SECTION 366 OF CR.PC.] [2.36]

Time limit for submission of death sentence proceedings to High Court by Court of Sessions

- Section 366 of Cr.PC provided that when the Court of session passes a death sentence, the proceedings shall be submitted to the High Court for confirmation and sentence shall be executed only after confirmation of the High Court

- Section 407 modifies this requirement by providing that when the Court of session passes a death sentence, the proceedings shall be *forthwith* submitted to the High Court for confirmation of the death sentence

DIRECTORATE OF PROSECUTION [SECTION 20 OF BNSS/ SECTION 25A OF Cr.PC.] [2.37]

District Directorate of Prosecution

- Section 20(1)(*b*) of BNSS provides that the State Government may establish District Directorate of Prosecution of every district consisting of as many Deputy Directors & Assistant Directors of Prosecution as it thinks fit

Eligible criteria of appointment of Director/Deputy Director of Prosecution

- Section 25A(2) of Cr.PC. provided that a person shall be eligible to be appointed as a Director of Prosecution or a Deputy Director of Prosecution, if he has been in practice as an advocate for not less than ten years and such appointment shall be made with concurrence of the Chief Justice of the High Court.
- Section 20(2)(*a*) of the BNSS has changed the eligibility criteria for appointment of a Director of Prosecution or a Deputy Director of Prosecution. Section 20(2) provides that a person shall be eligible to be appointed as a Director of Prosecution or a Deputy Director of Prosecution, if he has been in practice as an advocate for not less than fifteen years or is or has been a Sessions Judge
- Section 20 omits the requirement of concurrence of the Chief Justice of the High Court for appointment of a Director of Prosecution or a Deputy Director of Prosecution

Assistant Directors of Prosecution

- Section 20(2) creates new posts of Assistant Directors of Prosecution. Section 20(2)(*b*) provides that person shall be eligible to be appointed as an Assistant Director of Prosecution if he has been in practice as an advocate for not less than seven years or has been a Magistrate of the first class
- Assistant Director shall be subordinate to Deputy Director of Prosecution

Roles and responsibilities of Director/Deputy Director/Assistant Director of Prosecution

- Unlike section 25A of Cr.PC, section 20 of BNSS provides clear roles for Director of Prosecution, Deputy Director of Prosecution and Assistant Director of Prosecution and does not leave it entirely to the discretion of State Government to specify their roles and responsibilities. The roles and responsibilities of these officials are as under:
  - The powers and functions of the Director of Prosecution shall be to monitor cases in which offences are punishable for ten years or more, or with life imprisonment, or with death, to expedite the proceedings and to give opinion on filing of appeals.
  - The powers and functions of the Deputy Director of Prosecution shall be to examine and scrutinise police report and monitor the cases in which offences are punishable for seven years or more, but less than ten years, for ensuring their expeditious disposal.
  - The functions of the Assistant Director of Prosecution shall be to monitor cases in which offences are punishable for less than seven years.
  - The Director, Deputy Director or Assistant Director of Prosecution shall have the power to deal with and be responsible for all proceedings under this Sanhita.
  - The other powers and functions of the Director of Prosecution, the Deputy Directors of Prosecution and Assistant Director of Prosecution and the areas for which each of the Deputy Directors of Prosecution or Assistant Director of Prosecution have been appointed shall be such as the State Government may, by notification, specify.

DISCHARGE, PROCEDURE WHERE ACCUSED IS NOT DISCHARGED [SECTION 269 OF BNSS/SECTION 246 OF Cr.PC.] [2.38]

Closure of prosecution evidence where attendance of PWs cannot be secured despite giving opportunity to the prosecution and after taking all reasonable measures under this Sanhita

- **New sub-section (7) of section 269** of BNSS provides that where, despite giving opportunity to the prosecution and after taking all reasonable measures under this Sanhita, if the attendance of the prosecution witnesses under sub-sections (5) and (6) of section 269 cannot be secured for cross examination, it shall be deemed that such witness has not been examined for not being available, and the Magistrate may close the prosecution evidence for reasons to be recorded in writing and proceed with the case on the basis of the materials on record **[NEW]**

DISCHARGE, WHEN ACCUSED SHALL BE DISCHARGED [SECTION 262 OF BNSS/ SECTION 239 OF Cr.PC.] [2.39]

Time limit of application for discharge by accused

- The accused may prefer an application for discharge within a period of *sixty* days from the date of supply of copies of document under section 230. There was no such provision in section 239 of Cr.PC

Examination of accused through audio-video electronic means

- Accused can be examined either physically or through audio-video electronic means

ELECTRONIC COMMUNICATION [SECTION 2(*1*)(*i*) OF BNSS] [2.40]

Electronic communication

- "Electronic communication" means—
  - the communication of any written, verbal, pictorial information or video content transmitted or transferred
  - whether from one person to another, or from one device to another or from a person to a device or from a device to a person
  - by means of an electronic device including a telephone, mobile phone, or other wireless telecommunication device, or a computer, or audio-video players or cameras or any other electronic device or electronic form as may be specified by notification, by the Central Government

EVIDENCE FOR DEFENCE [SECTION 266 OF BNSS/SECTION 243 OF Cr.PC.] [2.41]

Examination of witness by audio-video electronic means

- New second proviso to section 266(2) of the BNSS provides that the examination of witness may be done by audio-video electronic means at the designated place to be notified by the State Government.

EVIDENCE FOR PROSECUTION [SECTION 265 OF BNSS/ SECTION 242 OF Cr.PC.] [2.42]

Recording of evidence of witness by audio-video electronic means

- New proviso to section 265 of BNSS provides that evidence of witness may be recorded by audio-video electronic means at the designated place to be notified by the State Government

EVIDENCE, MODE OF TAKING, EVIDENCE TO BE TAKEN IN PRESENCE OF ACCUSED [SECTION 308 OF BNSS/SECTION 273 OF Cr.PC.] [2.43]

Audio-video electronic means

- Section 308 of BNSS provides that except as otherwise expressly provided, all evidence taken in the course of the trial or other proceeding shall be taken in the presence of the accused, or, when his personal attendance is dispensed with, in the presence of his *advocate including through audio-video electronic means at the designated place to be notified by the State Government*

EVIDENCE, MODE OF TAKING, RECORD OF EXAMINATION OF ACCUSED [SECTION 316 OF BNSS/SECTION 281 OF Cr.PC.] [2.44]

Time limit for taking signature of accused examined by electronic communication

- Proviso to section 316(4) of BNSS provides that where the accused is in custody and is examined through electronic communication, his signature shall be taken within 72 hours of such examination

FORENSIC EVIDENCE COLLECTION FOR SERIOUS OFFENCES, MANDATORY [SECTION 176 OF BNSS/SECTION 157 OF CR.PC.] [2.45]

Forensic evidence collection centre

- Section 176(3) is a new provision. It mandates forensic teams to visit the crime scene to collect evidence for offences punishable by imprisonment of seven years or more.
- Section 176(3) of BNSS provides that on receipt of every information relating to the commission of an offence which is made punishable for seven years or more, the officer in charge of a police station shall, from such date, as may be notified within a period of five years by the State Government in this regard, cause the forensics expert to visit the crimes scene to collect forensic evidence in the offence and also cause videography of the process on mobile phone or any other electronic device.
- Where forensics facility is not available in respect of any such offence, the State Government shall, until the facility in respect of that matter is developed or made in the State, notify the utilisation of such facility of any other State.
- Section 157 of Cr. PC did not contain such a provision.

HANDWRITING, SIGNATURE SPECIMEN, POWER OF MAGISTRATE TO ORDER PERSON TO GIVE SPECIMEN SIGNATURES OR HANDWRITING, ETC. [SECTION 349 OF BNSS/ SECTION 311A OF Cr.PC.] [2.46]

Magistrate's power to order any person to give specimen signature, etc.

- Section 349 of BNSS empowers the Magistrate to order any person to give specimen signatures or handwriting or voice sample or finger impressions.
- Magistrate may, for reasons to be recorded in writing, order any a person to give such specimen without him being arrested

IN CAMERA TRIAL [SECTION 366 OF BNSS/SECTION 327 OF Cr.PC.] [2.47]

In camera trial provision extended to offences under Protection of Children from Sexual Offences Act also

- Section 327 of Cr.PC provided that inquiry into and trial of offences of rape and gang rape shall be *in camera*. Section 366 of BNSS provides that inquiry into and trial of rape or an offence under Protection of Children from Sexual Offences Act shall also be conducted *in camera*. [*See* Sections 4, 6, 8 and 10 of POCSO]

INVESTIGATION [SECTION 2(1)(*l*) OF BNSS/SECTION 2(*h*) OF Cr.PC.] [2.48]

Investigation

- New *Explanation* inserted in section 2(*1*)(*l*) of BNSS clarifies that where any of the provisions of a special Act as regards investigation are inconsistent with the provisions of this Sanhita, the provisions of the special Act shall prevail

JUDGMENT [SECTION 392 OF BNSS/SECTION 353 OF Cr.PC.] [2.49]

Time limit for pronouncing judgment by Court

- Section 392(1) of BNSS provides that the judgment in every trial in any Criminal Court or original jurisdiction shall be pronounced in open Court by the presiding officer immediately after the termination of the trial or at some subsequent time not later than *45 days* of which notice shall be given to the parties or their advocates. No such time limit was there in section 253 of Cr.PC

Time-limit for loading copy of Court's Judgment on its portal

- New proviso to section 392(4) provides that the Court shall, as far as practicable, upload the copy of the judgment on its portal within a period of *7 days* from the date of judgment

Accused in custody to hear judgment by audio-video electronic means

- If the accused is in custody, he shall be brought up to hear the judgment pronounced either in person or through audio-video electronic means

MAGISTRATE, COGNIZANCE OF OFFENCES BY [SECTION 210 OF BNSS/SECTION 190 OF Cr.PC.] [2.50]

Mode of taking cognizance

- Section 190 of Cr.PC specifies three modes of taking cognizance:

- Upon receiving a complaint of facts.
- Upon a police report.
- Upon information received from any person other than a police officer or upon the Magistrate's own knowledge.

◆ Section 210 of BNSS retains the same three modes of taking cognizance but adds the term "including any complaint filed by a person authorised under any special law" in the first mode.

◆ It also explicitly mentions that police reports can be recorded in any mode, including digital mode

MAGISTRATE, EXAMINATION OF COMPLAINANT [SECTION 223 OF BNSS/SECTION 200 OF Cr.PC.] [2.51]

Cognizance of complaint

◆ Section 200 of Cr.PC provided as under:

- a Magistrate taking cognizance of an offence on complaint shall examine upon oath the complainant and the witnesses present, if any, and
- the substance of such examination shall be reduced to writing and shall be signed by the complainant and the witnesses, and also by the Magistrate.

◆ Section 223 of BNSS makes two changes to above provisions as under:

- The first proviso to section 223(1) provides that no cognizance of an offence shall be taken by the Magistrate without giving the accused an opportunity of being heard.
- **New sub-section (2) of section 223** provides that a Magistrate shall not take cognizance on a complaint against a public servant for any offence alleged to have been committed in course of the discharge of his official functions or duties unless— **[NEW]**

  (*a*) such public servant is given an opportunity to make assertions as to the situation that led to the incident so alleged; and

  (*b*) a report containing facts and circumstances of the incident from the officer superior to such public servant is received.

MERCY PETITION IN DEATH SENTENCE CASES [SECTION 472 OF BNSS] [2.52]

Mercy petition

- ***Section 472 of BNSS is a new provision.*** **[NEW]**
- Section 472 of the BNSS provides for Mercy petition in death sentence cases. Section 472 provides as under:
  - A convict under the sentence of death or his legal heir or any other relative may, if he has not already submitted a petition for mercy, file a mercy petition before the President of India under article 72 or the Governor of the State under article 161 of the Constitution within a period of thirty days after the date on which the Superintendent of the Jail,—

    (*i*) informs him about the dismissal of the appeal or special leave to appeal by the Supreme Court; or

    (*ii*) informs him about the date of confirmation of the sentence of death by the High Court and the time allowed to file an appeal or special leave in the Supreme Court has expired
  - The petition may, initially be made to the Governor and on its rejection or disposal by the Governor, the petition shall be made to the President within a period of sixty days from the date of rejection or disposal of his petition.
  - The Superintendent of the Jail or officer in charge of the Jail shall ensure, that every convict, in case there are more than one convict in a case, also makes the mercy petition within a period of sixty days and on non-receipt of such petition from the other convicts, Superintendent of the Jail shall send the names, addresses, copy of the record of the case and all other details of the case to the Central Government or State Government for consideration along with the said mercy petition.
  - The Central Government shall, on receipt of the mercy petition seek the comments of the State Government and consider the petition along with the records of the case and make recommendations to the President in this behalf, as expeditiously as possible, within a period of sixty days from the date of receipt of comments of the State Government and records from Superintendent of the Jail.

- The President may, consider, decide and dispose of the mercy petition and, in case there are more than one convict in a case, the petitions shall be decided by the President together in the interests of justice.
- Upon receipt of the order of the President on the mercy petition, the Central Government shall within forty-eight hours, communicate the same to the Home Department of the State Government and the Superintendent of the Jail or officer in charge of the Jail.
- No appeal shall lie in any Court against the order of the President made under article 72 of the Constitution and it shall be final, and any question as to the arriving of the decision by the President shall not be enquired into in any Court.

METROPOLITAN AREA/METROPOLITAN MAGISTRATE [SECTION 6 OF BNSS/SECTION 6 OF Cr.PC.] [2.53]

Metropolitan Magistrate

- Concepts of 'Metropolitan Area' & 'Metropolitan Magistrate' are now abolished.

OFFENCE COMMITTED OUTSIDE INDIA [SECTION 208 OF BNSS/ SECTION 188 OF Cr.PC.] [2.54]

Offence committed outside India

- Section 188 of Cr.PC provided that offender (Indian Citizen committing offence anywhere outside India or a foreign national committing offence on an Indian Ship/aircraft) may be dealt with in respect of offence committed outside India as if it had been committed at any place within India at which he may be found
- Section 208 of BNSS provides that such offender may be dealt with in respect of offence committed outside India as if it had been committed at any place within India at which he may be found or where the *offence is registered in India*
- In section 208(1) of BNSS words "or where the offence is registered in India" are added at end.

ONLINE FIR [SECTION 173 OF BNSS/SECTION 154 OF Cr.PC.] [2.55]

Online FIR for cognizable offences: Information of cognizable offence can be given to Police by Electronic communication

- Section 154(1) of Cr.PC. contained no provision for enabling information relating to the commission of a cognizable offence to be given to an officer in charge of a police station by electronic communication.
- Section 173(1) of BNSS allows the information relating to the commission of a cognizable offence to be given to an officer in charge of a police station by electronic communication. In such a case, it shall be taken on record by him on being signed within three days by the person giving it. The substance of such electronic communication shall be entered in a book to be kept by such officer in such form as the State Government may prescribe in this behalf.
- In section 154 of Cr.PC. there was no option or provision to give information relating to the commission of a cognizable offence to be given to an officer in charge of a police station by electronic communication.

PLEA BARGAINING, APPLICATION FOR PLEA BARGAINING [SECTION 290 OF BNSS/ SECTION 265B OF Cr.PC.] [2.56]

Time-limit for filing application for plea bargaining

- Section 290 of BNSS fixes a time limit for filing of application of plea bargaining by the accused. Such application must be filed within a period of *thirty* days from the date of framing of charge in the Court. There was no such time-limit in existing provisions of section 265B of Cr.PC

Time-limit for reaching a mutually satisfactory disposition

- Section 265B did not provide any limit on the time the Court may allow for the Public Prosecutor/Complainant and accused to work out a mutually satisfactory disposition. Section 290 of BNSS provides that Court will allow time not exceeding *60 days* for the Public Prosecutor/Complainant and accused to work out a mutually satisfactory disposition

PLEA BARGAINING, DISPOSAL OF CASE [SECTION 293 OF BNSS/ SECTION 265E OF Cr.PC.] [2.57]

First time offender

- Section 265E of Cr.PC. contained provisions as to how Court will dispose of the case where a mutually satisfactory disposition of the case has been worked out by Public Prosecutor/Complainant and accused.
- Section 293 of BNSS makes changes to these provisions to require the Court to show leniency towards first-time offenders who opt for plea bargaining.
- Section 265E(*a*) of Cr.PC. provides that the Court shall award the compensation to the victim in accordance with the disposition under section 265D and hear the parties on the quantum of the punishment, releasing of the accused on probation of good conduct or after admonition under section 360 or for dealing with the accused under the provisions of the Probation of Offenders Act, 1958 or any other law for the time being in force and follow the procedure specified in the succeeding clauses for imposing the punishment on the accused.
- Section 293(*a*) of BNSS provides that the Court shall award the compensation to the victim in accordance with the disposition under section 292 and hear the parties on the quantum of the punishment, releasing of the accused on probation of good conduct or after admonition under section 401 or for dealing with the accused under the provisions of the Probation of Offenders Act, 1958 or any other law for the time being in force and follow the procedure specified in the succeeding clauses for imposing the punishment on the accused.
- Section 265E(*b*) of Cr.PC. provides that after hearing the parties under clause (*a*), if the Court is of the view that section 360 or the provisions of the Probation of Offenders Act, 1958 or any other law for the time being in force are attracted in the case of the accused, it may release the accused on probation or provide the benefit of any such law, as the case may be.
- Section 293(*b*) of BNSS provides that after hearing the parties under clause (*a*), if the Court is of the view that section 401 or the provisions of the Probation of Offenders Act, 1958 or any other law for the time being in force are attracted in the case of the accused, it may release the accused on probation or provide the benefit of any such law.

- Section 265E(*c*) of Cr.PC. provides that after hearing the parties under clause (*b*), if the Court finds that minimum punishment has been provided under the law for the offence committed by the accused, it may sentence the accused to *half* of such minimum punishment.
- Section 293(*c*) of BNSS provides that after hearing the parties under clause (*b*), if the Court finds that minimum punishment has been provided under the law for the offence committed by the accused, it may sentence the accused to half of such minimum punishment, *and where the accused is a first-time offender and has not been convicted of any offence in the past, it may sentence the accused to one-fourth of such minimum punishment*.
- Section 265E(*d*) of Cr.PC. provides that in case after hearing the parties under clause (*b*), the Court finds that the offence committed by the accused is not covered under clause (*b*) or clause (*c*), then, it may sentence the accused to one-fourth of the punishment provided or extendable, as the case may be, for such offence.
- Section 293(*d*) of BNSS provides that in case after hearing the parties under clause (*b*), the Court finds that the offence committed by the accused is not covered under clause (*b*) or clause (*c*), then, it may sentence the accused to one-fourth of the punishment provided or extendable, as the case may be, for such offence *and where the accused is a first-time offender and has not been convicted of any offence in the past, it may sentence the accused to one-sixth of the punishment provided or extendable, as the case may be, for such offence.*

POLICE, CASES TO BE SENT TO MAGISTRATE, WHEN EVIDENCE IS SUFFICIENT [SECTION 190 OF BNSS/SECTION 170 OF Cr.PC.] [2.58]

Security for appearance

- Section 170 of Cr.PC provided that if, upon an investigation under this Chapter, it appears to the officer in charge of the police station that there is sufficient evidence or reasonable ground as aforesaid, such officer shall forward the accused under custody to a Magistrate empowered to take cognizance of the offence upon a police report and to try the accused or commit him for trial, or, if the offence is bailable and the accused is able to give security, shall take security from him for his appearance before such Magistrate on a day fixed and for his attendance from day to day before such Magistrate until otherwise directed.

- Section 190 of BNSS makes a change to these provisions.
- Proviso below section 190(1) provides that if the accused is not in custody, the police officer shall take security from such person for his appearance before the Magistrate and the Magistrate to whom such report is forwarded shall not refuse to accept the same on the ground that the accused is not taken in custody.

POLICE, INFORMATION TO, INFORMATION AS TO NON-COGNIZABLE CASES AND INVESTIGATION OF SUCH CASES [SECTION 174 OF BNSS/SECTION 155 OF Cr.PC.] [2.59]

Daily Diary

- Section 155(1) of Cr.PC provided that when information is given to an officer in charge of a police station of the commission within the limits of such station of a non-cognizable offence, he shall enter or cause to be entered the substance of the information in a book to be kept by such officer in such form as the State Government may prescribe in this behalf, and refer the informant to the Magistrate.
- Section 174 of BNSS further requires such officer to forward the daily diary report of all such cases fortnightly to the Magistrate.

POLICE, INFORMATION TO, INFORMATION IN COGNIZABLE CASES [SECTION 173 OF BNSS/ SECTION 154 OF Cr.PC.] [2.60]

Introduction of "Zero FIRs" for Cognizable offences

- Section 173(1) of the BNSS facilitates the filing of "Zero FIRs" for offences occurring outside the jurisdiction of a police station but within the State.
- Section 173(1) provides that every information relating to the commission of a cognizable offence may be given orally or by electronic communication to an officer in charge of a police station

Online FIR for cognizable offences: Information of cognizable offence can be given to Police by Electronic communication

- Section 154(1) of Cr.PC contained no provision for enabling information relating to the commission of a cognizable offence to be given to an officer in charge of a police station by electronic communication

- Section 173(1) of BNSS allows the information relating to the commission of a cognizable offence to be given to an officer in charge of a police station by electronic communication. In such a case, it shall be taken on record by him on being signed within three days by the person giving it. The substance of such electronic communication shall be entered in a book to be kept by such officer in such form as the State Government may prescribe in this behalf.
- In section 154 of Cr.PC, there was no option or provision to give information relating to the commission of a cognizable offence to be given to an officer in charge of a police station by electronic communication.

Information to informant/victim

- Section 154(2) required copy of information recorded to be given forthwith, free of cost, to the informant. Section 173(2) requires a copy to be so given to the informant or the victim.

Preliminary enquiry **[NEW]**

- ***Section 173(3) is a new provision.*** It provides that without prejudice to the provisions contained in section 175, on receipt of information relating to the commission of any cognizable offence, which is made punishable for three years or more but less than seven years, the officer in-charge of the police station may with the prior permission from an officer not below the rank of Deputy Superintendent of Police, considering the nature and gravity of the offence,—

  (*i*) proceed to conduct preliminary enquiry to ascertain whether there exists a *prima facie* case for proceeding in the matter within a period of fourteen days; or

  (*ii*) proceed with investigation when there exists a *prima facie* case.

- There was no provision along these lines in section 154 of Cr.PC.

Powers of Superintendent of Police

- Section 173(4) of the BNSS provides that any person aggrieved by a refusal on the part of an officer in charge of a police station to record the information referred to in sub-section (1), may send the substance of such information, in writing and by post, to the Superintendent of Police concerned who, if satisfied that such information discloses the commission of a cognizable offence, shall either investigate the case himself or direct an investigation to be made by any police officer subordinate to him, in the manner provided by this Sanhita, and such officer shall have all the powers of an officer in charge of the police station in relation to that offence *failing which he may make an application under sub-section (3) of section 175 to the Magistrate*. Words in italics depicts the additional provision which was not there in section 154(4) of Cr.PC.

POLICE, MEDICAL EXAMINATION OF VICTIM OF RAPE [SECTION 184 OF BNSS/SECTION 164A OF Cr.PC.] [2.61]

Time-limit for submission of medical examination report of rape victim

- Section 184 of BNSS incorporates the provisions of section 164A with one difference. Section 184 makes the submission of medical examination report by RMP time-bound by requiring that medical examination report be forwarded to the investigating officer within a period of *seven days*. Hitherto, existing provisions required that registered medical practitioner shall, "without delay" forward the report to the investigating officer and fixed no time limit.

POLICE, PERSONS BOUND TO CONFORM TO LAWFUL DIRECTIONS OF POLICE [SECTION 172 OF BNSS] [2.62]

Binding force of lawful directions of Police

- ***Section 172 of the BNSS is a new provision.*** **[NEW]**
- Section 172 of BNSS provides as under:
  - All persons shall be bound to conform to the lawful directions of a police officer given in fulfilment of any of his duty under this Chapter [Chapter XII of BNSS dealing with Preventive Action of the Police].
  - A police officer may detain or remove any person resisting, refusing, ignoring or disregarding to conform to any direction given by him as above and may either take such person before a Judicial Magistrate or, in petty cases, release him as soon as possible within a period of 24 hours.

Mandatory Forensic Evidence Collection for Serious Offences [NEW]

- Section 176(3) is a new provision. It mandates forensic teams to visit the crime scene to collect evidence for offences punishable by imprisonment of seven years or more.
- Section 176(3) of BNSS provides that on receipt of every information relating to the commission of an offence which is made punishable for seven years or more, the officer in charge of a police station shall, from such date, as may be notified within a period of five years by the State Government in this regard, cause the forensics expert to visit the crimes scene to collect forensic evidence in the offence and also cause videography of the process on mobile phone or any other electronic device.
- Where forensics facility is not available in respect of any such offence, the State Government shall, until the facility in respect of that matter is developed or made in the State, notify the utilisation of such facility of any other State.
- Section 157 of Cr.PC did not contain such a provision.

Non-compliance with requirement of section 176(1)

- Section 176(1) of BNS provides that if, from information received or otherwise, an officer in charge of a police station has reason to suspect the commission of an offence which he is empowered under section 175 to investigate, he shall forthwith send a report of the same to a Magistrate empowered to take cognizance of such offence upon a police report and shall proceed in person, or shall depute one of his subordinate officers not being below such rank as the State Government may, by general or special order, prescribe in this behalf, to proceed, to the spot, to investigate the facts and circumstances of the case, and, if necessary, to take measures for the discovery and arrest of the offender:

  Provided that—

  (*a*) when information as to the commission of any such offence is given against any person by name and the case is not of a serious nature, the officer in charge of a police station need not proceed in person or depute a subordinate officer to make an investigation on the spot;

  (*b*) if it appears to the officer in charge of a police station that there is no sufficient ground for entering on an investigation, he shall not investigate the case.
- Section 176(2) of BNSS [corresponding to section 157(2) of Cr.PC] additionally provides that when officer in-charge of Police

Station has not fully complied with the requirement of first proviso to section 176(1) [requirement to proceed to the crime spot to make an investigation or depute a subordinate officer to do so], he shall state reasons for such non-followance (why and how case is of non-serious nature/why he opines that there is no sufficient ground for entering into an investigation) and forward the daily diary report to Magistrate. Such report shall also be sent to informant in case of non-compliance with clause (*b*) of first proviso to section 176(1).

POLICE, POWER TO SUMMON PERSONS [SECTION 195 OF BNSS/ SECTION 175 OF Cr.PC.] [2.67]

Restrictions on power to summon persons

- Section 175(1) of Cr.PC provided as under:
  - A police officer proceeding under section 174 (Police to enquire and report on suicide, etc.) may, by order in writing, summon two or more persons as aforesaid for the purpose of the said investigation, and any other person who appears to be acquainted with the facts of the case and
  - Every person so summoned shall be bound to attend and to answer truly all questions other than questions the answers to which would have a tendency to expose him to a criminal charge or to a penalty or forfeiture.
- Section 195(1) of BNSS makes a change to the above provisions. Proviso to section 195(1) provides that no male person under the age of fifteen years or above the age of sixty years or a woman or a mentally or physically disabled person or a person with acute illness shall be required to attend at any place other than the place where such person resides, unless such person is willing to attend and answer at the police station or at any other place within the limits of such police station.

POLICE, PROCEDURE WHEN INVESTIGATION CANNOT BE COMPLETED IN 24 HOURS [SECTION 187 OF BNSS/SECTION 167 OF Cr.PC.] [2.68]

Period of declaration

- Section 167(2) of Cr.PC provided that the Magistrate to whom an accused person is forwarded under this section may, whether he has or has not jurisdiction to try the case, from time to time, authorise the detention of the accused in such custody as such Magistrate thinks fit, for a term not exceeding fifteen days in the whole; and if he has no jurisdiction to try the case or commit it for trial, and considers further detention unnecessary, he may order the accused to be forwarded to a Magistrate having such jurisdiction.

- Section 187(2) of BNSS provides that the Magistrate to whom an accused person is forwarded under this section may, irrespective of whether he has or has no jurisdiction to try the case, after taking into consideration the status of the accused person as to whether he is not released on bail or his bail has not been cancelled, authorise, from time to time, the detention of the accused in such custody as such Magistrate thinks fit, for a term not exceeding fifteen days in the whole, or in parts, at any time during the initial forty days or sixty days out of detention period of sixty days or ninety days, as the case may be, as provided in sub-section (3) of section 187, and if he has no jurisdiction to try the case or commit it for trial, and considers further detention unnecessary, he may order the accused to be forwarded to a Judicial Magistrate having such jurisdiction.

Detention in police station

- Second proviso to section 187(5) provides that no person shall be detained otherwise then in police station under police custody or in prison under Judicial custody or place declared as prison by the Central/State Government.

Audio-video electronic means

- Words 'audio-video electronic means' have replaced the words 'medium of electronic video linkage' which were used in section 167 of Cr.PC.

POLICE, RECORDING OF CONFESSIONS AND STATEMENTS [SECTION 183 OF BNSS/SECTION 164 OF Cr.PC.] [2.69]

Woman Magistrate

- Newly inserted first proviso to section 183(6)(*a*) provides that statement of rape victim/gang rape victim/acid attack victim shall, as far as practicable, be recorded by a woman Magistrate and in her absence by a male Magistrate in the presence of a woman.

Recording statement of witness

- Newly inserted second proviso to section 183(6)(*a*) provides that in cases relating to the offences punishable with imprisonment for ten years or more or imprisonment for life or with death, the Magistrate shall record the statement of the witness brought before him by the police officer.

Audio-video electronic means

- Fourth proviso to section 183(6)(*a*) provides that where the person making the statement is temporarily or permanently mentally or physically disabled, the statement made by the person, with the assistance of an interpreter or a special educator, shall be recorded through audio-video electronic means preferably by mobile phone instead of the existing requirement that the statement be videographed.

POLICE, REPORT OF POLICE OFFICER ON COMPLETION OF INVESTIGATION [SECTION 193 OF BNSS/SECTION 173 OF Cr.PC.] [2.70]

Requirement of time-bound completion of investigation within 2 months applicable to offences of rape and gang rape have been extended to offences under POCSO

- Hitherto, section 173 of Cr.PC provided for time-bound completion of Police investigation into *offence under section 376, 376A, 376AB, 376B, 376C, 376D, 376DA, 376DB or 376E of the Indian Penal Code (offences of rape and gang rape)*.
- Investigation into offences of rape and gang rape were required to be completed within 2 months from the date on which information was recorded by officer in charge of Police Station.
- Section 193(2) extends this requirement to offences under Provisions of Protection of Children from Sexual Offences Act also [*See* sections 4, 6, 8, 10 and 12 of POCSO, 2012]

Electronic communication

- Section 193(3)(*i*) of BNSS provides that report to Magistrate can also be forwarded through electronic communication.
- Sub-clause (*i*) of section 193(3)(*i*) of BNSS provides that report shall also contain 'the sequence of custody in case of electronic device'.

Progress of investigation

- Section 193(3)(*ii*) of BNSS provides that the police officer shall within 90 days inform the progress of investigation by any means including electronic communication to informant or the victim.

Mandatory Submission of copies of documents to Magistrate by investigating officer for supply of the same to accused

- Section 173(7) of Cr.PC provided that where the police officer investigating the case finds it convenient so to do, he may furnish to the accused copies of all or any of the following documents:
  - (*a*) all documents or relevant extracts thereof on which the prosecution proposes to rely other than those already sent to the Magistrate during investigation;
  - (*b*) the statements recorded under section 161 of Cr.PC (Section 180 of BNSS) of all the persons whom the prosecution proposes to examine as its witnesses.
- Section 193(8) of BNSS makes the following changes to above provisions:
  - Section 193(8) makes it obligatory for Police Officer investigating the case to submit such number of copies of the police report along with other documents duly indexed to the Magistrate for supply to the accused as required under section 230. The words "where the police officer investigating the case finds it convenient so to do, he may furnish" have been replaced with the words "shall also submit".
  - Supply of report and other documents by electronic communications shall be considered as duly served.

Time-limit for completion of investigation

- Proviso to section 193(9) of BNSS provides that further investigation during the trial may be conducted with the permission of the Court trying the case and same shall be completed within a period of 90 days which may be extended with the permission of Court.

POLICE REPORT, SUPPLY TO ACCUSED OF COPY OF POLICE REPORT AND OTHER DOCUMENTS [SECTION 230 OF BNSS/ SECTION 207 OF Cr.PC.] [2.71]

Time limit stipulated for supply of copy of police report, FIR etc.

- Section 207 of Cr.PC provided that in any case where the proceeding has been instituted on a police report, the Magistrate shall *without delay* furnish to the accused, free of cost, a copy of each of the following:—
  - (*i*) the police report;

(*ii*) the first information report recorded under section 154;

(*iii*) the statements recorded under sub-section (3) of section 161 of all persons whom the prosecution proposes to examine as its witnesses, excluding therefrom any part in regard to which a request for such exclusion has been made by the police officer under sub-section (6) of section 173;

(*iv*) the confessions and statements, if any, recorded under section 164;

(*v*) any other document or relevant extract thereof forwarded to the Magistrate with the police report under sub-section (5) of section 173.

- Section 230 of BNSS requires the above documents to be supplied free of cost to the accused without *any delay*, and in no case beyond *14 days* from the date of production or appearance of the accused.
- ***The words "without delay" have been replaced by the words "without delay, and in no case beyond fourteen days from the date of production or appearance of the accused".***

Copy to victim

- Supply of police report and other documents free of cost within 14 days is to be made to the accused and the *victim* also if victim is represented by an advocate.

Report in electronic form

- Supply of documents in electronic form shall be considered as duly furnished.

PROCLAIMED OFFENDER, IDENTIFICATION AND ATTACHMENT OF PROPERTY OF PROCLAIMED PERSON [SECTION 86 OF BNSS] [2.72]

Attachment of property **[NEW]**

- ***This is a new provision. There was no corresponding provision in Cr.PC.***
- Section 86 of BNSS provides that the Court may, on the written request from a police officer not below the rank of the Superintendent of Police or Commissioner of Police, initiate the process of requesting assistance from a Court or an authority in the contracting State for identification, attachment and forfeiture of property belonging to a proclaimed person in accordance with the procedure provided in Chapter VIII.

PROCLAIMED OFFENDER, INQUIRY, TRIAL OR JUDGMENT IN ABSENTIA OF PROCLAIMED OFFENDER [SECTION 356 OF BNSS] [2.73]

- ***Section 356 of BNSS is a new provision*** **[NEW]**
- Section 356 provides as follows:

1. When a person declared as a proclaimed offender, whether or not charged jointly, has absconded to evade trial and there is no immediate prospect of arresting him,

- it shall be deemed to operate as a waiver of the right of such person to be present and tried in person, and
- the Court shall, after recording reasons in writing, in the interest of justice, proceed with the trial in the like manner and with like effect as if he was present and pronounce the judgment.

The Court shall not commence the trial unless a period of 90 days has lapsed from the date of framing of the charge.

2. The Court shall ensure that the following procedure has been complied with before proceeding under (1) above namely:—

(*i*) issuance of execution of two consecutive warrants of arrest within the interval of atleast thirty days;

(*ii*) publish in a national or local daily newspaper circulating in the place of his last known address of residence, requiring the proclaimed offender to appear before the Court for trial and informing him that in case he fails to appear within thirty days from the date of such publication, the trial shall commence in his absence;

(*iii*) inform his relative or friend, if any, about the commencement of the trial; and

(*iv*) affix information about the commencement of the trial on some conspicuous part of the house or homestead in which such person ordinarily resides and display in the police station of the district of his last known address of residence.

3. Where the proclaimed offender is not represented by any advocate, he shall be provided with an advocate for his defence at the expense of the State.

4. Where the Court, competent to try the case or commit for trial, has examined any witnesses for prosecution and recorded their depositions, such depositions shall be given in evidence against such proclaimed offender on the inquiry into, or in trial for, the offence with which he is charged.

   If the proclaimed offender is arrested and produced or appears before the Court during such trial, the Court may, in the interest of justice, allow him to examine any evidence which may have been taken in his absence.

5. Where a trial is related to a person under this section:
   - the deposition and examination of the witness, may, as far as practicable, be recorded by audio-video electronic means preferably mobile phone and
   - such recording shall be kept in such manner as the Court may direct.

6. In prosecution for offences under this Sanhita, voluntary absence of accused after the trial has commenced under (1) above shall not prevent continuing the trial including the pronouncement of the judgment even if he is arrested and produced or appears at the conclusion of such trial.

7. No appeal shall lie against the judgment under this section unless the proclaimed offender presents himself before the Court of appeal.

   No appeal against conviction shall lie after the expiry of three years from the date of the judgment.

8. The State may, by notification, extend the provisions of this section to any absconder mentioned in section 84(1) of this Sanhita.

Deemed Joint Trial [Section 24 of BSA]

- New *Explanation II* is added in section 24 of Bharatiya Sakshya Adhiniyam, 2023 so as to clarify that "A trial of more persons than one held in the absence of the accused who has absconded or who fails to comply with a proclamation issued under section 84 of the Bharatiya Nagarik Suraksha Sanhita, 2023 shall be deemed to be a joint trial for the purpose of this section."

PROCLAIMED OFFENDER - POLICE, DUTY OF OFFICERS EMPLOYED IN CONNECTION WITH AFFAIRS OF A VILLAGE

TO MAKE A CERTAIN REPORT [SECTION 34 OF BNSS/ SECTION 40 OF Cr.PC.] [2.74]

Proclaimed offender

- Section 40(2)(*ii*) of Cr.PC defined 'proclaimed offender' with reference to specific provisions of IPC.
- Section 34 of the BNSS defines 'proclaimed offender' to include any person proclaimed as an offender by any Court or authority in any territory in India to which BNSS does not extend, in respect of any act which if committed in the territories to which BNSS extends, would be an offence punishable under any of the offence *punishable with imprisonment for ten years or more or with imprisonment for life or with death* under the Bharatiya Nyaya Sanhita, 2023.

PROPERTY, DISPOSAL OF, ORDER FOR CUSTODY AND DISPOSAL OF PROPERTY PENDING TRIAL IN CERTAIN CASES [SECTION 497 OF BNSS/SECTION 451 OF Cr.PC.] [2.75]

Magistrate

- Besides any Criminal Court, Magistrate can make an order under section 497(1) of BNSS [Section 497(1) of BNSS]

Statement of property

- The Court or the Magistrate shall, within a period of fourteen days from the production of the property before it, prepare a statement of such property containing its description in such form and manner as the State Government may, by rules, provide. [Section 497(2) of BNSS]

Photograph/videography of property

- The Court or the Magistrate shall cause to be taken the photograph and if necessary, videograph on mobile phone or any electronic media, of such property [Section 497(3) of BNSS]
- The statement prepared as above and the photograph or the videography taken as above shall be used as evidence in any inquiry, trial or other proceeding under the Sanhita. [Section 497(4) of BNSS]

Time limit for disposal of property

- The Court or the Magistrate shall, within a period of thirty days after the statement has been prepared and the photograph or the videography has been taken, order the disposal, destruction, confiscation or delivery of the property in the manner specified hereinafter. [Section 497(5) of BNSS]

PROPERTY, POWER TO SELL PERISHABLE PROPERTY [SECTION 505 OF BNSS/SECTION 459 OF Cr.PC.] [2.76]

Prescribed value

- Section 459 of Cr.PC provided that if the person entitled to the possession of such property is unknown or absent and the property is subject to speedy and natural decay, or if the Magistrate to whom its seizure is reported is of opinion that its sale would be for the benefit of the owner, or that the value of such property is less than *five hundred rupees*, the Magistrate may at any time direct it to be sold.
- Section 505 modifies the above provisions by increasing the limit for value of perishable property from ₹ 500 to ₹ 10,000 by replacing the words "is less than five hundred rupees" with the words "is less than ten thousand rupees".

PROSECUTION, WITHDRAWAL FROM [SECTION 360 OF BNSS/ SECTION 321 OF Cr.PC.] [2.77/78]

Opportunity of hearing to victim before allowing withdrawal of prosecution

- New second proviso to section 360 of BNSS provides that no court shall allow withdrawal from prosecution by Public Prosecutor without giving an opportunity of being heard to the victim in the case

PUBLIC NUISANCE, MAGISTRATE MAY PROHIBIT THE REPETITION OR CONTINUANCE OF PUBLIC NUISANCE [SECTION 162 OF BNSS/SECTION 143 OF Cr.PC.] [2.79]

Deputy Commissioner of Police

- Section 143 of Cr.PC provides that a District Magistrate or Sub-divisional Magistrate, or any other Executive Magistrate empowered by the State Government or the District Magistrate in this behalf, may order any person not to repeat or continue a public nuisance

- Besides any other Executive Magistrate, under section 162 of BNSS, a Deputy Commissioner of Police may also be empowered by the State Government or District Magistrate to order any person not to repeat or continue a public nuisance and such DCP can also issue such an order. This modification intends to reduce workload on Executive Magistrates

PUBLIC NUISANCE, PERSON TO WHOM ORDER IS ADDRESSED TO OBEY OR SHOW CAUSE [SECTION 154 OF BNSS/SECTION 135 OF Cr.PC.] [2.80]

Audio video conference

- Section 135 of Cr.PC provided that the person against whom conditional order for removal of nuisance is made shall (*a*) obey the order; or (*b*) appear in accordance with such order and show cause against the same
- Section 154 of BNSS has made changes to these provisions to allow such person to show cause through audio video conferencing instead of appearing in person and showing cause

PUBLIC NUISANCE, PROCEDURE WHERE PERSON AGAINST WHOM ORDER IS MADE APPEARS TO SHOW CAUSE [SECTION 157 OF BNSS/SECTION 138 OF Cr.PC.] [2.81]

Time-limit for completion of proceedings

- Section 138 of Cr.PC contained provisions regarding procedure to be followed where person against whom conditional order for removal of nuisance is made appears in court to show cause
- Section 157 of BNSS has made changes to these provisions to make this procedure time-bound. Section 157 of BNSS provides that the proceedings under this section shall be completed, as soon as possible, within a period of ninety days, which may be extended for the reasons to be recorded in writing, to one hundred and twenty days

PUBLIC ORDER AND TRANQUILITY, DISPERSAL OF ASSEMBLY BY USE OF CIVIL FORCE [SECTION 148 OF BNSS/SECTION 129 OF Cr.PC.] [2.82]

Provision made gender neutral

- Section 129 of Cr.PC empowered the Executive Magistrate or Officer-in-charge of Police Station or any Police Officer not below the rank of sub-inspector (in absence of such officer in charge) to require the assistance of any *male* person for dispersing unlawful assembly where it does not disperse on being commanded to disperse.
- Section 148 of BNSS has replaced the words "any male person" with the words "any person" so as to empower the Executive Magistrate or Police Officer to take assistance of any person irrespective of gender of such person.

PUBLIC ORDER AND TRANQUILITY, USE OF ARMED FORCES TO DISPERSE ASSEMBLY [SECTION 149 OF BNSS/SECTION 130 OF Cr.PC.] [2.83]

District/Executive Magistrate

- Section 130 of Cr.PC empowered the *Executive Magistrate of the highest rank* present to cause unlawful assembly to be dispersed by the armed forces.
- Section 149 of the BNSS has changed these provisions to empower *District Magistrate or any other Executive Magistrate authorised by him*, who is present, to cause unlawful assembly to be dispersed by the armed forces.

PUBLIC PROSECUTORS [SECTION 18 OF BNSS/SECTION 24 OF Cr.PC.] [2.84]

Public prosecutors for National Territory of Delhi Region

- New proviso to section 18(1) of BNSS provides that the Central Government shall appoint the Public Prosecutor or Additional Public Prosecutors for the National Capital Territory of Delhi after consultation with the High Court of Delhi

Special Public Prosecutor

- Under BNSS, the definition of "Prosecuting Officer" includes a Special Public Prosecutor also

PUBLIC SERVANTS, EVIDENCE OF PUBLIC SERVANTS, EXPERTS, PUBLIC OFFICERS IN CERTAIN CASES [SECTION 336 OF BNSS] [2.85]

Successor officer/expert

- ***Section 336 of the BNSS is a new provision.*** **[NEW]**
- Section 336 provides that where any document or report prepared by a public servant, scientific expert, medical officer or investigating officer is purported to be used as evidence in any inquiry, trial or other proceeding under this Sanhita, and—

  (*i*) such public servant, expert or officer is either transferred, retired, or died; or

  (*ii*) such public servant, expert or officer cannot be found or is incapable of giving deposition; or

  (*iii*) securing presence of such public servant, expert or officer is likely to cause delay in holding the inquiry, trial or other proceeding,

  the Court shall secure presence of successor officer of such public servant, expert, or officer who is holding that post at the time of such deposition to give deposition on such document or report.

PUBLIC SERVANT, PROSECUTION FOR CONTEMPT OF LAWFUL AUTHORITY OF PUBLIC SERVANTS, FOR OFFENCES AGAINST PUBLIC JUSTICE AND FOR OFFENCES RELATING TO DOCUMENTS GIVEN IN EVIDENCE [SECTION 215 OF BNSS/ SECTION 195 OF Cr.PC.] [2.86]

Cognizance by whom

- Section 195(1) of Cr.PC provided for cognizance of offences of contempt of lawful authority of public servants, for offences against public justice and for offences relating to documents given in evidence, on complaint in writing of the public servant concerned or of some other public servant to whom he is *administratively subordinate*

- Section 215(1) of BNSS has modified these provisions so as enable cognizance on complaint in writing of public servant concerned or some other public servant *who is authorised by the concerned public servant* so to do

PUBLIC SERVANT, PROSECUTION OF JUDGES AND PUBLIC SERVANTS [SECTION 218 OF BNSS/SECTION 197 OF Cr.PC.] [2.87]

Time limit for sanction

- Section 218 of BNSS provides that government shall take a decision within a period of 120 days from the date of the receipt of the request for sanction and in case it fails to do so, the sanction shall be deemed to have been accorded by such Government. [2nd proviso to Section 218(1)]

SEARCH, MOBILE RECORDING [SECTION 185 OF BNSS/SECTION 165 OF Cr.PC.] [2.88]

Mandatory Recording of search by mobile phone

- Proviso to section 185(2) of BNSS stipulates a new requirement which makes it compulsory to record the search conducted through audio-video electronic means preferably by mobile phone.

Time limit for sending records

- Sub-section (5) of section 185 of BNSS provides that copies of record made under section 185(1)/(3) shall forthwith, but not later than 48 hours, be sent to Magistrate.
- No such time-limit was there in section 165 of Cr.PC.

SEARCH, MOBILE RECORDING, AUDIO VIDEO ELECTRONIC MEANS, RECORDING OF SEARCH AND SEIZURE THROUGH AUDIO-VIDEO ELECTRONIC MEANS [SECTION 105 OF BNSS] [2.89]

Recording of search & seizure by mobile phone

- ***Section 105 is a new provision. There was no corresponding requirement or provision in Cr.PC*** **[NEW]**

- Section 105 provides that the process of conducting search of a place or taking possession of any property, article or thing, including preparation of the list of all things seized in the course of such search and seizure and signing of such list by witnesses, shall be recorded through any audio-video electronic means preferably cell phone and the police officer shall without delay forward such recording to the District Magistrate, Sub-divisional Magistrate or Judicial Magistrate of the first class.

SECURITY FOR GOOD BEHAVIOUR FROM HABITUAL OFFENDERS [SECTION 129 OF BNSS/SECTION 110 OF Cr.PC.] [2.90]

Specified Acts

- Section 110 of Cr.PC empowered Executive Magistrate to require a habitual offender under one or more of the following Acts to show cause why he should not be ordered to execute a bond, with sureties, for his good behaviour for such period, not exceeding three years, as the Magistrate thinks fit:
  - the Drugs and Cosmetics Act, 1940;
  - the Foreign Exchange Regulation Act, 1973;
  - the Employees' Provident Fund and Family Pension Fund Act,1952;
  - the Prevention of Food Adulteration Act, 1954;
  - the Essential Commodities Act, 1955;
  - the Untouchability (Offences) Act, 1955;
  - the Customs Act, 1962; and
  - the Foreigners Act, 1946.

SENTENCE COMMUTATION OF, POWER TO COMMUTE SENTENCE [SECTION 474 OF BNSS/SECTION 433 OF Cr.PC.] [2.91]

Commutation of sentences

- Section 433 of Cr.PC empowered the Appropriate Government to commute sentences without the consent of the accused. Section 474 of BNSS corresponds to section 433 of Cr.PC

  The comparison between section 433 and section 474 is tabulated below:

Sentence	*What the sentence in Col. (1) may be commuted for by appropriate Govt. under section 433 of Cr.PC*	*What the sentence in Col.(1) may be commuted for by appropriate Govt. under section 474 of BNSS*
(1)	*(2)*	*(3)*
Sentence of death	Appropriate Government may commute a death sentence for any other punishment provided by the Indian Penal Code	Death sentence may be commuted for imprisonment for life
A sentence of imprisonment for life	Sentence may be commuted for imprisonment for a term not exceeding fourteen years or for fine	Sentence may be commuted for imprisonment for a term not less than 7 years
A sentence for imprisonment for seven or more years	—	Sentence may be commuted for imprisonment for a term not less than 3 years
A sentence of rigorous imprisonment	Sentence may be commuted for simple imprisonment for any term to which that person might have been sentenced, or for fine	Sentence may be commuted for simple imprisonment for any term to which that person might have been sentenced
A sentence of simple imprisonment	Sentence may be commuted for fine	—
Sentence for imprisonment for less than seven years	—	Sentence may be commuted for fine

SENTENCES, IN CASES OF CONVICTION OF SEVERAL OFFENCES AT ONE TRIAL [SECTION 25 OF BNSS/SECTION 31 OF Cr.PC.] [2.92]

Court to clearly spell out in order whether punishments to run consecutively or concurrently after considering the gravity of the offences

- Section 31 of Cr.PC provided that when a person is convicted at one trial of two or more offences, the Court may sentence him for such offences to the several punishments prescribed therefor which such Court is competent to inflict. Section 31 further provided that such punishments when consisting of imprisonment to commence the one after the expiration of the other in such order as the Court may direct, unless the Court directs that such punishments shall run concurrently.

- Section 25 of BNSS provides that when a person is convicted at one trial of two or more offences, the Court may, subject to the provisions of section 9 of BNS, sentence him for such offences to the several punishments prescribed therefor which such Court is competent to inflict. Section 25 requires the Court to clearly order such punishments to run consecutively or concurrently after considering the gravity of offences.

Maximum punishment for imprisonment for life

- Maximum punishment is increased from 14 years to 20 years

SENTENCES, WHICH HIGH COURTS AND SESSIONS JUDGES MAY PASS [SECTION 22 OF BNSS/SECTION 28 OF Cr.PC.] [2.93]

Assistant Sessions Judge

- Power of Assistant Sessions Judge to pass sentences in section 28(3) of Cr.PC has been omitted by section 22 of the BNSS

SENTENCES, WHICH MAGISTRATES MAY PASS [SECTION 23 OF BNSS/SECTION 29 OF Cr.PC.] [2.94]

Monetary limits on fines

- The monetary limits on fines which can be imposed by Judicial Magistrates of First class and Judicial Magistrates of second class have been enhanced by the BNSS as under:

Class of Criminal Court	*Monetary limit under section 29 of Cr.PC on fine that Court can impose*	*Revised enhanced monetary limits under section 23 of BNSS on the fine that Court can impose*
The Court of a Judicial Magistrate of the first class	Fine not exceeding ₹ 10,000	Fine not exceeding ₹ 50,000

Class of Criminal Court	*Monetary limit under section 29 of Cr.PC on fine that Court can impose*	*Revised enhanced monetary limits under section 23 of BNSS on the fine that Court can impose*
The Court of a Judicial Magistrate of the second class	Fine not exceeding ₹ 5,000	Fine not exceeding ₹ 10,000

Metropolitan Area/Metropolitan Magistrate

- Concepts as to 'Metropolitan Area' & 'Metropolitan Magistrate' are abolished

Community Service

- Section 23 of BNSS empowers a Magistrate to pass a sentence of community service.
- "Community service" shall mean the work which the Court may order a convict to perform as a form of punishment that benefits the community, for which he shall not be entitled to any remuneration.
- To reduce the burden on jails, community service has been included in BNS as a punishment for the first time and it is being given legal status. [*PIB Press Release, dated 20-12-2023*]

Offences for which punishment of community service can be awarded

- Bharatiya Nyaya Sanhita, 2023 prescribes *Community Service* as punishment for petty offences
- Under BNS, Community service, *inter alia,* can be awarded as punishment in case of following offences:

Section of BNS	*Offence*
Section 202	Public servant unlawfully engaging in trade.
Section 209	Non-appearance in response to a proclamation under section 84 of Bharatiya Nagarik Suraksha Sanhita, 2023.
Section 226	Attempt to commit suicide to compel or restraint exercise of lawful power.
Proviso below section 303(2)	In cases of theft where the value of the stolen property is less than five thousand rupees, and a person is convicted for the first time,

Section of BNS	*Offence*
	shall upon return of the value of property or restoration of the stolen property, shall be punished with community service.
Section 355	Misconduct in public by a drunken person.
Section 356	Defamation

SPECIAL EXECUTIVE MAGISTRATES [SECTION 15 OF BNSS/ SECTION 21 OF Cr.PC.] [2.95]

Police Officer

◆ Besides Executive Magistrate, State Government can also appoint any police officer not below the rank of Superintendent of Police or equivalent to be known as Special Executive Magistrate

SUMMARY TRIALS, POWER TO TRY SUMMARILY [SECTION 283 OF BNSS/SECTION 260 OF Cr.PC.] [2.96]

Mandatory Summary trial for petty and less serious cases

◆ Section 283 of BNSS makes summary trial *mandatory* for petty and less serious cases. Under Cr.PC, it was *discretionary* for the Magistrate to try petty and less serious offences in a summary way as section 260(1) of Cr.PC uses the words "may, if he thinks fit, try in a summary way all or any of the following offences". Section 283(1) of BNSS replaces the word "may" with the word "shall" and has also increased monetary limits from ₹ 2000 to ₹ 20000 for petty offences to be tried summarily. The comparison of Cr.PC provisions and BNSS provisions on summary trial are given below in the following Table:

Chapter XXI of Cr.PC	*Chapter XXII of BNSS*
Section 260(1) (1) Notwithstanding anything contained in this Code— (*a*) any Chief Judicial Magistrate; (*b*) any Metropolitan Magistrate;	**Section 283(1)** (1) Notwithstanding anything contained in this Sanhita— (*a*) any Chief Judicial Magistrate; (*b*) Magistrate of the first class,

Chapter XXI of Cr.PC	*Chapter XXII of BNSS*
(*c*) any Magistrate of the first class specially empowered in this behalf by the High Court, *may*, **if he thinks fit, try in a summary way** all or any of the following offences:— (*i*) offences not punishable with death, imprisonment for life or imprisonment for a term exceeding two years; [Section 260(1)] (*ii*) theft, where the value of the property stolen does not exceed ₹ *2000*; (*iii*) receiving or retaining stolen property, where the value of the property does not exceed ₹ *2000*; (*iv*) assisting in the concealment or disposal of stolen property, where the value of such property does not exceed ₹ *2000*; (*v*) offences under sections 454 and 456 of the Indian Penal Code; (*vi*) insult with intent to provoke a breach of the peace, and criminal intimidation punishable with imprisonment for a term which may extend to two years, or with fine, or with both; (*vii*) abetment of any of the foregoing offences;	***shall try in a summary way*** all or any of the following offences:— (*i*) theft, where the value of the property stolen does not exceed ₹ *20000*; (*ii*) receiving or retaining stolen property, where the value of the property does not exceed ₹ *20000*; (*iii*) assisting in the concealment or disposal of stolen property, where the value of such property does not exceed ₹ *20000*; (*iv*) offences under section 330 of the Bharatiya Nyaya Sanhita, 2023; (*v*) insult with intent to provoke a breach of the peace, and criminal intimidation, under section 349 of the Bharatiya Nyaya Sanhita, 2023; (*vi*) abetment of any of the foregoing offences; (*vii*) an attempt to commit any of the foregoing offences, when such attempt is an offence; (*viii*) any offence constituted by an act in respect of which a complaint may be made under section 20 of the Cattle-trespass Act, 1871. [Section 283(1)]

Chapter XXI of Cr.PC	Chapter XXII of BNSS
(*viii*) an attempt to commit any of the foregoing offences, when such attempt is an offence; (*ix*) any offence constituted by an act in respect of which a complaint may be made under section 20 of the Cattle-trespass Act, 1871. [Section 260(1)]	

- **New sub-section (2) of section 283 of the BNSS** provides that the Magistrate may, after giving the accused a reasonable opportunity of being heard, for reasons to be recorded in writing, try in a summary way all or any of the offences not punishable with death or imprisonment for life or imprisonment for a term exceeding three years.

  No appeal shall lie against decision of Magistrate to try a case in a summary way. **[NEW]**

SUMMONS, FORM OF [SECTION 63 OF BNSS/SECTION 61 OF Cr.PC.] [2.97]

Electronic summons

- Section 61 of Cr.PC provided that every summons issued by a Court shall be in writing, in duplicate, signed by the presiding officer of such Court or by such other officer as the High Court may, from time to time, by rule direct, and shall bear the seal of the Court. The extant provisions do not provide for summons in electronic form.
- Section 63 of BNSS allows the Court to issue summons in an encrypted or any other form of electronic communication with the image of the seal of the Court or digital signature.

SUMMONS, HOW SERVED [SECTION 64 OF BNSS/SECTION 62 OF Cr.PC] [2.98]

Summons by electronic communication

- Section 62 of Cr.PC did not provide for service of summons by electronic communication.

- Proviso to section 64(2) of BNSS provides that summons bearing the image of Court's seal may also be served by electronic communication in such form and in such manner, as the State Government may, by rules, provide.

Record keeping

- Proviso to section 64(1) of BNSS requires that the Police Station or the registrar in the Court shall maintain a register to enter the address, e-mail address, phone number or such other details as the State Government by rules provided

SUMMONS, ISSUE OF PROCESS [SECTION 227 OF BNSS/SECTION 204 OF Cr.PC.] [2.99]

Electronic summons

- New proviso to section 227(1) of the BNSS provides that summons or warrants may also be issued through electronic means.

SUMMONS, NON-APPEARANCE OR DEATH OF COMPLAINANT [SECTION 279 OF BNSS/SECTION 256 OF Cr.PC.] [2.100]

Acquittal of accused for non-appearance of complainant

- If summons issued on complaint and complainant does not appear on day fixed for hearing or any subsequent day to which hearing is adjourned to, the Magistrate may, after giving 30 days time to the complainant to be present, acquit the accused. These provisions also apply when non-appearance is due to death of complainant. No such time-limit was there in section 256 of Cr.PC

SUMMONS, PROOF OF SERVICE IN SUCH CASES AND WHEN SERVING OFFICER NOT PRESENT [SECTION 70 OF BNSS/SECTION 68 OF Cr.PC.] [2.101]

Summons by electronic communication

- Section 70 of BNSS retains existing provisions of section 68 of Cr.PC. It further provides that all summons served through electronic communication under sections 64 to 71 of BNSS shall be considered as duly served and a copy of such electronic summons shall be attested and kept as a proof of service of summons. Section 68 of Cr.PC did not provide that summons served through electronic communication shall be considered as duly served.

SUMMONS, SERVICE OF SUMMONS ON CORPORATE BODIES, FIRMS AND SOCIETIES [SECTION 65 OF BNSS/SECTION 63 OF Cr.PC.] [2.102]

Service of summons to firm, or association of individuals other than company or corporation

- "Company" means a body corporate and "corporation" means an incorporated company or other body corporate or a society registered under the Societies Registration Act, 1860.
- Section 65(2) of BNSS provides that service of a summons on a firm or other association of individuals may be effected by serving it on any partner of such firm or association, or by letter sent by registered post addressed to such partner, in which case the service shall be deemed to have been effected when the letter would arrive in ordinary course of post.

SUMMONS, SERVICE OF SUMMONS ON WITNESS [SECTION 71 OF BNSS/SECTION 69 OF Cr.PC.] [2.103]

Summons by electronic communication

- Section 71 of BNSS provides that a Court issuing a summons to a witness may, in addition to and simultaneously with the issue of such summons, direct a copy of the summons to be served by *electronic communication* or by registered post addressed to the witness at the place where he ordinarily resides or carries on business or personally works for gain.
- On the proof of delivery of summons under sub-section (3) of section 70 of BNSS by electronic communication to the satisfaction of the Court, the Court issuing summons may deem that the summons had been duly served.

SUMMONS, SUBSTANCE OF ACCUSATION TO BE STATED [SECTION 274 OF BNSS/SECTION 251 OF Cr.PC.] [2.104]

Release of accused [NEW]

- **New proviso to section 274** requires that if the Magistrate considers the accusation as groundless, he shall, after recording the reasons in writing, release the accused. Such release shall have the effect of discharge. This is a new requirement which was not there in corresponding provision of section 251 of Cr.PC

TRIAL AND PROCEEDINGS TO BE HELD IN ELECTRONIC MODE [SECTION 530 OF BNSS] [2.105]

- ***Section 530 is a new provision. There were no corresponding provisions in Cr.PC*** **[NEW]**
- Section 530 of the BNSS relates to trial and proceedings to be held in electronic mode.
- This section provides that trials and proceedings under this Code, may be held in electronic mode, by use of electronic communication or use of audio-video electronic means
- Section 530 provides that all trials, inquires and proceedings under this Sanhita, including—
  - (*i*) summons and warrant, issuance, service and execution thereof;
  - (*ii*) holding of inquiry;
  - (*iii*) examination of complainant and witnesses;
  - (*iv*) trial before a Court of Session, trial in warrant cases, trial in summons-cases, summary trials and plea bargaining;
  - (*v*) recording of evidence in inquiries and trials;
  - (*vi*) trials before High Courts;
  - (*vii*) all appellate proceedings and such other proceedings,

  may be held in electronic mode, by use of electronic communication or use of audio-video electronic means.

VICTIMS, TREATMENT OF [SECTION 397 OF BNSS/SECTION 357C OF Cr.PC.] [2.106]

Duty of hospitals to provide immediately, the first-aid or medical treatment, free of cost to victims of offences under Protection of Children from Sexual Offences Act, 2012

- A duty was cast on hospitals u/s 357C of Cr.PC to provide immediately, the first-aid or medical treatment, free of cost, to the victims of offences of rape, gang rape and acid attack

- Section 397 of BNSS extends the scope of above duty of hospitals to also provide first-aid or medical treatment, free of cost, to the victims of offences under sections 4, 6, 8 or section 10 of the Protection of Children from Sexual Offences Act, 2012 also.

WITNESS EXAMINATION, NO FORMAL PROOF OF CERTAIN DOCUMENTS [SECTION 330 OF BNSS/SECTION 294 OF Cr.PC.] [2.107]

Time-limit for acceptance or denial of genuineness of document

- Where any document is filed before any Court by the prosecution or the accused, the particulars of every such document shall be included in a list and the prosecution or the accused or the advocate for the prosecution or the accused, if any, shall be called upon to admit or deny the genuineness of each such document soon after supply of such documents and *in no case later than 30 days after such supply. The Court may, in its discretion, relax the time limit with reasons to be recorded in writing*

Expert

- Second proviso to section 330(1) of BNSS provides that no expert shall be called to appear before the Court unless the report of such expert is disputed by any of the parties to the trial

WITNESS PROTECTION SCHEME [SECTION 398 OF BNSS] [2.108]

Protection of witness

- ***Section 398 of BNSS is a new provision.*** **[NEW]**
- Section 398 of BNSS provides that every State Government shall prepare and notify a witness protection scheme for the State with a view to ensure protection of the witnesses.

ZERO FIRs [SECTION 173 OF BNSS/SECTION 154 OF Cr.PC] [2.109]

Introduction of "Zero FIRs" for Cognizable offences

- Section 173(1) of the BNSS facilitates the filing of "Zero FIRs" for offences occurring outside the jurisdiction of a police station but within the State.
- Section 173(1) provides that every information relating to the commission of a cognizable offence may be given orally or by electronic communication to an officer in charge of a police station

DIVISION THREE

UNDERSTANDING LAW OF EVIDENCE UNDER BHARATIYA SAKSHYA ADHINIYAM, 2023 (BSA)

ALPHABETICAL KEY TO UNDERSTANDING LAW OF EVIDENCE UNDER BHARATIYA SAKSHYA ADHINIYAM, 2023 (BSA)

Relevancy of statement as to fact of public nature contained in certain acts or notifications, ***para 3.11***

- Official Gazette in electronic or digital form

Relevancy of statements as to any law contained in law books including electronic or digital form, ***para 3.12***

- E-books/Websites

Secondary evidence, ***para 3.13***

- Secondary evidence

Short title, application and commencement, ***para 3.14***

- Territorial extent of the legislation
- Applicability to Courts-martial

UNDERSTANDING LAW OF EVIDENCE UNDER BHARATIYA SAKSHYA ADHINIYAM, 2023 (BSA)

CONSIDERATION OF PROVED CONFESSION AFFECTING PERSON MAKING IT AND OTHERS JOINTLY UNDER TRIAL FOR SAME OFFENCE [SECTION 24 OF BSA/SECTION 30 OF EVIDENCE ACT] [3.1]

Joint Trial

- *Explanation* to section 30 of Evidence Act incorporated in section 24 of BSA is renumbered as *Explanation I*
- New *Explanation II* is added in section 24 of BSA so as to clarify that "A trial of more persons than one held in the absence of the accused who has absconded or who fails to comply with a proclamation issued under section 84 of the Bharatiya Nagarik Suraksha Sanhita, 2023 (BNSS) shall be deemed to be a joint trial for the purpose of this section."

DOCUMENT [SECTION 2(*1*)(*d*) OF BSA/SECTION 3, PARA 5, OF EVIDENCE ACT] [3.2]

Electronic & digital records

- Section 2(*1*)(*d*) of BSA gives a new definition of the word "document" which is compatible with the modern digital era.
- The new definition specifically includes electronic and digital records within the scope of the term "document".
- An electronic record on emails, server logs, documents on computers, laptop or smartphone, messages, websites, locational evidence and voice mail messages stored on digital devices are documents.

- Under the new definition, to qualify as "document" or "documentary evidence", it is not necessary that matter be expressed or described upon any substance by means of letters, figures or marks only.
- Any matter which is "otherwise recorded" upon any substance "by any other means" will also qualify as "document" or "documentary evidence". Therefore, video recording on mobile phone would qualify as "documentary evidence" as it is "otherwise recorded" upon any substance "by any other means".

ELECTRONIC OR DIGITAL RECORD [SECTION 61 OF BSA] [3.3]

Electronic records

- Section 61 of BSA provides that electronic or digital record shall have the same legal effect, validity and enforceability as paper records.
- Section 61 of BSA provides that nothing in the Adhiniyam shall apply to deny the admissibility of an electronic or digital record in the evidence on the ground that it is an electronic or digital record and such record (subject to section 63 of BSA) shall have the same legal effect, validity and enforceability as other documents.

ELECTRONIC RECORDS, ADMISSIBILITY OF [SECTION 63 OF BSA/SECTION 65B OF EVIDENCE ACT] [3.4]

Scope of provision

- Section 63 of BSA uses the words "computer or any communication device" for words "computer"
- Section 65B(1) of Evidence Act provided that any information contained in an electronic record which is printed on a paper, stored, recorded or copied in optical or magnetic media produced by a computer (the computer output) shall be deemed to be also a document, if the specified conditions are satisfied in relation to the information and computer in question and shall be admissible in any proceedings, without further proof or production of the original, as evidence of any contents of the original or of any fact stated therein of which direct evidence would be admissible.

Section 63(1) of BSA extends the scope of above provision to make it applicable also to any information contained in semiconductor memory or in any communication device (e.g. smartphone) or otherwise stored, recorded or copied in any electronic form.

- Format of certificate under section 63(4) which is to accompany electronic record evidence is specified in Schedule to BSA. There was no such format specified in Evidence Act for certificate in section 65B(4).

EVIDENCE [SECTION 2(*1*)(*e*) OF BSA/SECTION 3, PARA 6, OF EVIDENCE ACT] [3.5]

Electronic/Digital records

- Under the new definition of "evidence" in section 2(1)(*e*) of the BSA, 'statements including statements given electronically' are to be treated as evidence as well as oral evidence. This is a logical corollary to section 530 of Bharatiya Nagarik Suraksha Sanhita, 2023 (BNSS) providing for examination of complainant and witnesses in electronic mode by use of electronic communication or by audio-video electronic means.
- Under Evidence Act, only electronic records were treated as documentary evidence and there was no express mention of digital records in definition of 'evidence' under Evidence Act.
- Section 2(*1*)(*e*) of BSA specifically includes electronic or digital records as documentary evidence.

PRESUMPTION AS TO ELECTRONIC AGREEMENTS [SECTION 85 OF BSA/SECTION 85A OF EVIDENCE ACT] [3.6]

Digital signature

- Section 85A of Evidence Act provided that the Court shall presume that every electronic record purporting to be an agreement containing the electronic signatures of the parties was so concluded by affixing the electronic signature of the parties.
- Section 85 of BSA provides that the Court shall presume that every electronic record purporting to be an agreement containing the electronic or digital signature of the parties was so concluded by affixing the electronic or digital signature of the parties.

PRESUMPTION AS TO GAZETTES IN ELECTRONIC OR DIGITAL RECORD [SECTION 81 OF BSA/SECTION 81A OF EVIDENCE ACT] [3.7]

Digital records

- Section 81A of Evidence Act provided that the Court shall presume the genuineness of every electronic record purporting to be the Official Gazette. Section 81 of BSA provides that the Court shall presume the genuineness of every electronic or digital record purporting to be the Official Gazette.

Keeping of records

- Section 81A of Evidence Act provided that the Court shall presume the genuineness of every electronic record purporting to be electronic record directed by any law to be kept by any person, if such electronic record is kept substantially in the form required by law and is produced from proper custody. However, section 81A did not clarify as to what is proper custody.
- Section 81 of BSA provides that the Court shall presume the genuineness of every electronic or digital record purporting to be electronic or digital record directed by any law to be kept by any person, if such electronic or digital record is kept substantially in the form required by law and is produced from proper custody. Further, new *Explanation* in section 81 of BSA clarifies that "For the purposes of this section and section 96 electronic records are said to be in proper custody if they are in the place in which, and looked after by the person with whom such document is required to be kept; but no custody is improper if it is proved to have had a legitimate origin, or the circumstances of the particular case are such as to render that origin probable.".

PRIMARY EVIDENCE [SECTION 57 OF BSA/SECTION 62 OF EVIDENCE ACT] [3.8]

Electronic record

- New *Explanations* (*Explanation 4* to *Explanation 7*) are inserted in section 57 of BSA.
- New *Explanation 4* clarifies that where an electronic or digital record is created or stored, and such storage occurs simultaneously or sequentially in multiple files, each such file is primary evidence.

- New *Explanation 5* clarifies that where an electronic or digital record is produced from proper custody, such electronic and digital record is primary evidence unless it is disputed.
- New *Explanation 6* clarifies that where a video recording is simultaneously stored in electronic form and transmitted or broadcast or transferred to another, each of the stored recordings is primary evidence.
- New *Explanation* 7 clarifies that where an electronic or digital record is stored in multiple storage spaces in a computer resource, each such automated storage, including temporary files, is primary evidence.

PRODUCTION OF DOCUMENTS [SECTION 165 OF BSA/SECTION 162 OF EVIDENCE ACT] [3.9]

Communication between Ministers and President of India

- New proviso to section 165 of BSA provides that no Court shall require any communication between the Ministers and the President of India to be produced before it

RELEVANCY OF CERTAIN JUDGMENTS IN PROBATE, ETC., JURISDICTION [SECTION 35 OF BSA/SECTION 41 OF EVIDENCE ACT] [3.10]

Tribunal's Orders

- Tribunal's orders are now also covered in section 35 of BSA

RELEVANCY OF STATEMENT AS TO FACT OF PUBLIC NATURE CONTAINED IN CERTAIN ACTS OR NOTIFICATIONS [SECTION 31 OF BSA/SECTION 37 OF EVIDENCE ACT] [3.11]

Official Gazette in electronic or digital form

- Electronic or digital form of Official Gazette is made admissible evidence by section 31 of BSA

RELEVANCY OF STATEMENTS AS TO ANY LAW CONTAINED IN LAW BOOKS INCLUDING ELECTRONIC OR DIGITAL FORM [SECTION 32 OF BSA/SECTION 38 OF EVIDENCE ACT] [3.12]

E-books/Websites

- In certain circumstances electronic or digital form of law books as well as Court's rulings in electronic or digital form are now made admissible in evidence by section 32 of BSA
- Section 32 of BSA provides that when the Court has to form an opinion as to a law of any country, any statement of such law contained in a book purporting to be printed or published including in electronic or digital form under the authority of the Government of such country and to contain any such law, and any report of a ruling of the Courts of such country contained in a book including in electronic or digital form purporting to be a report of such rulings, is relevant.

SECONDARY EVIDENCE [SECTION 58 OF BSA/SECTION 63 OF EVIDENCE ACT] [3.13]

Secondary evidence

- Under section 58 of BSA Secondary evidence also includes:
  - oral admissions.
  - written admissions.
  - evidence of a person who has examined a document, the original of which consists of numerous accounts or other documents which cannot conveniently be examined in Court, and who is skilled in the examination of such documents.

SHORT TITLE, APPLICATION AND COMMENCEMENT [SECTION 1 OF BSA/SECTION 1 OF EVIDENCE ACT] [3.14]

Territorial extent of the legislation

- Section 1 of the Evidence Act provided that it extended to the whole of India. Section 1 of the BSA omits this provision on territorial extent. It also omits the definition of "India" given in section 3 of the Evidence Act.

- The possible reason for such omission is that any stipulation that the BSA extends to the whole of India would call into question the admissibility of evidence digitally generated outside the borders of India.

Applicability to Courts-martial

- Section 1 of the Evidence Act provided that the said Act did not apply to Courts-martial convened under the Army Act, the Naval Discipline Act or the Indian Navy (Discipline) Act or the Air Force Act.
- Section 1(2) of the BSA omits the words "convened under the Army Act, the Naval Discipline Act or the Indian Navy (Discipline) Act or the Air Force Act".
- Thus, unlike the Evidence Act, the BSA shall also apply to courts-martial convened under the Army Act, the Naval Discipline Act or the Indian Navy (Discipline) Act or the Air Force Act.

